. CHARISMA . CONTENT . CONCEPT

CONVERSATION
CONFIDENCE

OSMOND DESILVA

AND

ELIZABETH SMITH

HOW TO THRIVE IN ANY SOCIAL SETTING AND
NEVER RUN OUT OF THINGS TO SAY

Conversation Confidence

ISBN 978-1-908585-08-0

GOLD RUSH Publishing® books may be purchased for educational, business, or sales promotional use. We are an independent publishing house promoting innovative publications. For information please email: info@GoldRushPublishing.org.

Available for sale in bookshops, online at Amazon.com, and other channels worldwide.

Conversation Confidence

Contents

Introduction

Conversation is an art that everyone can master!

Everyone needs to learn to speak well in varying social situations. By "social situations" I mean not only attendance at a social event or gathering, but also being in the company of family and friends, in the workplace, in relationships and even in formal settings like an interview or speaking before the public.

Conversation has existed ever since humanity created language. Since then, certain styles of communication have always been with us, even if many of us may not be aware of this.

There are five core components of communication that we use nearly every time we communicate in a social setting. The five are listed below and will be explained in more depth in Chapters 1 to 5, accompanied with special exercises designed to help you understand and master them:

1. Story telling and story writing

2. Humour

3. Role-playing

4. Cold-readings

5. Connection and rapport

Other, supporting components also exist that we use in communication, but to a lesser extent, as will be explained in Chapters 6 to 10, namely:

6. Banter

7. Teasing

8. Questions and statements

9. Open loops and baited hooks

10. Multiple threads

We will use the term "outer game" to refer to the conversation we carry on in social situations. This term encompasses our body language and voice tonality as well as verbal behaviour. You can only improve your outer game if you understand what it means and what it is really about.

Chapters 11 to 18 give examples of the practical application of the theory covered in previous chapters.

By contrast, the term "inner game" refers to your own mind-set. It is of course closely related to your outer game, yet it is a distinct subject-matter of its own. The components of inner game will be covered in Chapters 19 to 29.

Below is a list of eight questions that people commonly ask when beginning to learn about their outer game:

1. *What is my outer game?*

Your outer game is the game you play with other people. It encompasses:

- everything you say in words, as well as

- body language and voice tonality.

Your outer game is affected and often determined by your inner game and by how you react to the people around you and the overall social environment.

2. How important is it compared to my inner game?

Your inner game will generally drive your outer game. Communication acts consist of non-verbal as well as verbal content. In terms of how much they determine the success of our communications, these aspects may be ranked as follows:

Non-verbal communication:

Inner game   60 %

Outer game, body language and voice tonality   30 %

Verbal communication:

Outer game, spoken words or content   10 %

All three aspects are important when meeting people and none of them should be underestimated.

3. Does how I talk matter as much as what I talk about?

Yes it does!

The manner in which you talk to people is more important than the content of what you say. Content is only the "end product", your hearers will want to get to know the person who is behind the content (*i.e.* emotions, thoughts, actions).

People are making assessments of you at all times by the way you "come across". For maximal effectiveness, your conversation needs to be:

- interesting,

- challenging, and

- different from that of other people

in order for you to be able to keep people engaged and to be memorable.

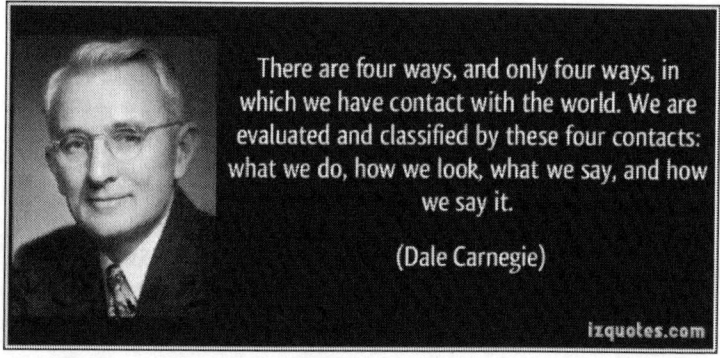

There are four ways, and only four ways, in which we have contact with the world. We are evaluated and classified by these four contacts: what we do, how we look, what we say, and how we say it.

(Dale Carnegie)

izquotes.com

4. How should I come across in a social situation?

At all times you have to be composed, comfortable and in control. Also, you should be the leader in the conversation. Speak and gesture slowly and listen carefully to what others have to say – be interested in them.

The quality of the conversation is more important than the quantity (*i.e.* avoid talking too much).

5. What should the content of my conversation consist of?

We carry on conversation for the sake of influence and persuasion, which is brought about by altering a person's emotional state. Ideally, in the content of your conversation you should be able to cover a wide range of emotions – happiness, sadness, jealousy, anger, *etc.*

The content ought to be, preferably:

- original and unique,

- creative and imaginative,

- showing an ability to think outside the box, and

- come from your own experience.

6. How do I alter another person's emotional state?

There are several ways to do this; you can:

(a) use highly detailed and descriptive language,

(b) get the person to visualise and imagine,

(c) let the person talk about his experiences, and

(d) turn the ordinary into the extraordinary.

7. Why do I run out of things to say and what should I do when this happens?

You run out of things to say when you lack familiarity and connection with the other person. You have lots to talk about with people you know well, like your family and friends. You can get over this "stranger-complex" by assuming familiarity and getting involved with more conversations with many different people.

If you do run out of things to say, you can:

- start a new thread/topic,

- ask another question,

- summarise what the other person has already said, or

- take a (short) break from the conversation.

8. How do I become a good conversationalist?

Getting proficient at conversation is akin to learning a language. Progress is made by following the 3 Ps (*i.e.* Practice, Piecemeal and Period).

You will need to practice this material over a period of time and in small piece.

You can also add to this mix the qualities of Patience, Persistence and being Proactive.

(Note that the words "he" and "she" can be used interchangeably in the text.)

1. Story telling and story writing

Story telling is probably the oldest art form and the most important conversation skill. We are always telling other people stories: narrations, anecdotes, tales, *etc*. Stories are capable of blending all aspects of communication seamlessly – the real with the surreal, fact with fiction, the past with the future and so on.

As with other skills, story telling needs to pack high emotional content and capture the imagination without delay within a short period of time. Your stories reflect your own experience and express the fact that you want to draw the listener into your reality. Your stock of stories needs to touch as wide a range of emotions as possible.

From women's perspective, the most important theme is romance and relationships. All romance novels, movies and television dramas are based on this theme. From a man's perspective, tales of bravery, courage, action heroes and leadership will always be of interest.

Structure of the story

From our earliest days we have known on some intuitive level that all effective stories have a three stage structure – a beginning, a middle and an end

i.e. a challenge, a struggle and a resolution.

Beginning	*Middle*	*End*
Challenge	Struggle	Resolution
Setup	Conflict	Conclusion

The timeline/frame of a story looks like this:

Change in character(s) and plot

Action > > > > > > > > > > > > > > > > > Goal

Motivation of main character to
achieve goal by taking action

It is the main characters who drive the plot and make the story come alive. The story develops over time through significant changes in the characters as the plot unfolds. The main characters strive toward a goal (which both they and we may be unaware of, setting up an element of surprise) and they reach the goal by taking action and getting involved with other characters along the way.

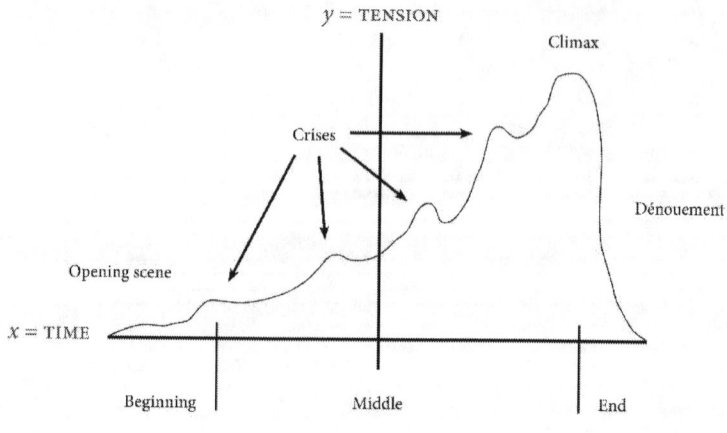

Hooks

A hook is a statement you use in order to grab the listener's attention and redirect it onto the story track. It is the bridge and transition from other topics of conversation to your story's beginning. A hook must intrigue the listener by creating both interest and suspense as to what you will say next.

The most well-known hook is,

> "Once upon a time . . ."

But, there are many other hooks you can use, such as:

> "This reminds me of the time when . . ."

> "Have you ever been to Japan?" (this is a "you" hook)

> "Have you ever eaten a burrito?" (this is another "you" hook)

> "You will never believe what happened . . ."

> "Last week I had the most amazing experience . . ."

> "Imagine a time when . . ." (this is a fantasy/fiction hook)

Set-up

A set-up is the introduction to a story, as every story must have a suitable beginning. You introduce the characters and set the scene with concrete details. The set-up must be brief yet it must contain sufficient information to lay a proper foundation for understanding the rest of the story.

The scene (including social background, location, environment, time, mood, atmosphere, dress) must reflect the theme of the story you are telling. For example:

- a horror story will be based in a spooky house or in an isolated area,

- a crime story will have an unsolved crime,

- a romance story will have a situation where a boy can meet a girl,

- a fantasy story will take place in some exotic realm of strange beings, and

- a period story will be based on a specific historical context.

Rather than giving logical facts and figures, you need to provide vivid descriptions, that invoke in the listener an "experience" of the location just as if he was one of the characters (see the section titled "Show, don't tell" below)

For example, you might lead into the story somehow like this:

> "It was growing cold and night was falling, much earlier than we expected. We could hear howls in the distance and the rippling of a nearby stream, but apart from that there was a dead silence. The only company we had was a blue full moon and a blazing camp fire."

Or instead of an atmosphere, you could begin with a sudden burst of action:

> "Amy was on her way to meet her best friend at the coffee shop. As she was withdrawing some cash from the machine, something suddenly startled her.

A man bolted past, chased along the high street by three policemen during morning rush hour. With a gun in one hand and a brief-case in the other, the fugitive forces his way through the crowds by firing bursts of bullets into the air. The exploding shots make passers-by scream and others flee for their lives.

As Amy stood transfixed, she saw the man push an old lady over as he leapt onto the back seat of a waiting motorbike, shouting to the driver, 'Go!'"

Notice how many simple, active verbs were used in just three short paragraphs: bolted, chase, force, fire, burst, explode, scream, flee, push, leap, shout.

The James Bond film "Goldeneye" begins with an action scene where Bond leaps off a dam. In the photo, stuntman Wayne Michaels, standing in as the Pierce Brosnan's double, leaps off the Verzasca Dam in Switzerland.

Characters

It is the characters who are the life of a story and give it a sense of meaning and purpose. The characters must be such that the listener can relate to them, and so they must have weaknesses and vulnerabilities as well as virtues. They must be assigned specific roles to act out, the significance of which becomes clear as the story unfolds (*e.g.* hero, heroine, villain).

A character must have a unique identity and personality for him to be believable. Among the most determinant characteristics that will identify him include his:

Name, age, country of origin, hobbies/interests, work/business, marital status, children, family/friends, personal and social background/history.

In order to make your character have a 3D image, he must have believable characteristics:

(a) **Appearance**
Bring out anything unique about the way the person looks.

(b) **Relationships**
With other people (*e.g.* family and friends) and his reactions to them.

(c) **Behaviour**
Including his faults, as well as all other habits, mannerisms, gestures and voice, his reaction to events and circumstances.

(d) **Thoughts**
This will include his likes/dislikes, secrets, memories, ambitions/aspirations/hopes.

(e) **Emotional state and feelings**
Which could give insight into his "dark side" – anger, hatred, jealousy, fears.

(f) **Strengths and weaknesses**
That is, lots of strong points and one or two weak ones.

(g) **Keep him mysterious**
To increase tension and suspense; therefore, do not put all of the foregoing on the table right away.

The character can be introduced or revealed in the story in five main ways:

- **Through description**
  By describing what they look like, what they wear, their lifestyle in general.

- **Through setting**
  By way of where the character lives, works and spends his spare time.

- **Through actions**
  By way of his behaviour, body language, gesture, facial expressions and mannerisms.

- **Through others**
  By his relationships with family, friends and acquaintances. This includes their view, opinions, judgements and reaction to that person.

- **Through dialogue**
  By his accent, speech, tone of voice and what he says.

You will need to explain the character's basic motivations as well as the specific reasons why he takes a certain course of action in his self-development (which is known as the "character arc").

Plot

The plot is a sequencing of events that like glue binds a story together. The underlying nature of plots may range from blazing action (like Hollywood movies) to a vehicle for heartfelt emotions (like a romance story). It may well be a combination of several of these types.

From the beginning you must have in mind a clear mission or goal for the hero or heroine which he or she can achieve by the end. Happy stories are the ones where the hero goes from a low to a high state, for example:

- rags to riches,

- unknown to being famous,

- lonely to being romantically fulfilled.

The goals must not be too easy and must confront the hero with plenty of challenges; at the same time, however, it must not be too hard and certainly not impossible. The challenges and obstacles create the tension or conflict in the story. You must bear in mind that your listeners or readers, will always be asking themselves:

(a) Will the hero ever achieve his goal?

(b) How will the hero ever achieve his goal?

(c) When will the hero ever achieve his goal?

A plot is a phase-shift of events over a period of time. It must have consequences for the characters involved in it, usually by way of "cause and effect" scenarios.

For example, this scenario of:

> "A man sitting at home playing with his computer or reading a book all day long . . ."

would not make for the plot of a successful story.

Now consider scenarios which, though may start with a man sitting at home, nonetheless have the makings of a good plot:

- he switches on the telly to hear news of an air accident that his friend is involved in, or

- he opens the door and accepts a parcel from a postman that has a rose in it, but no name.

To tell a story about your own life, you need to ask yourself questions like:

(a) What were the key defining moments in my life?

(b) Who were the most important people or role models in my life?

(c) At which point in my life did I change for the better (or worse) and why?

(d) What are the lessons I learned from my most formative experiences?

(e) What were my biggest fears in life and how did I overcome them?

You can make up short stories about recent events in your life by asking the generic question,

What was the:

- funniest,

- craziest,

- weirdest,

- most embarrassing,

- most interesting,

- most emotional,

- most memorable, and

- most loving,

event that happened to me in the past few days/weeks/months?

Conflict (*a.k.a.* drama or crisis)

Conflict is of the essence of a good plot, and it is this which creates the tension or intrigue that draws listeners in. The tension is released only when the conflict is finally resolved. Tension is created or heightened in two main ways:

(a) **Internal conflict**
(the hero *vs.* himself)
This is how a character's self-development and growth takes place.
For example, he is not satisfied with his life and wants to make a change for the better, but has to make a difficult moral choice, he cannot live with his secret past, having self-doubt,

and/or

(b) **External conflict**
(the hero *vs.* other people, thing and/or circumstances)

This is where the action that is visible to the world takes place.

For example, his plans are opposed by other people in the town where he lives, he must beat an opponent, things start going wrong in his life, *etc.*

At various points in the story the hero will have to make choices about which course of action to take. Since he cannot be perfect, any choice that he makes will result in some form of struggle before he will be able to reach his goal. The hero must always be faced with challenges and obstacles in life.

The conflict may be heightened in several ways by:

(a) **Empowerment**
Giving all sides choices/options even if the odds are stacked against them; or
The opponent/villain may also be brave, intelligent, harming and a match for the hero.

(b) **High stakes**
The listener must be convinced that the hero is on an important mission and must win or else catastrophe will ensue: *e.g.* he has only a limited time to stop a terrorist plot.

(c) **Consequences**
There must be a significant impact/effect on the hero himself as a result of his conduct: *e.g.* the bad guy gets beaten and the good guy gets rewarded.

(d) **Taking opposite sided of the same coin**
e.g. two good guys who ought to be friends find themselves unexpectedly at odds, the heroine wishes to preserve the forest, but the hero wishes to log it; or
An odd couple (*e.g.* a tidy person and an untidy person share the same room).

(e) **The rubber-band or yo-yo plot device**
The hero swings between nearly achieving his goal, then watching it slip away from him – this should be due to external conflict, but with the result that, his internal dialogue also swings from victory and hope to despair and disappointment.

(f) **Constraints of time and resources**
He does not have enough time to achieve the goal, or he does not have enough supporters to back his cause.

The first conflict that starts the story in motion is called the "incitement incident".

Mystery and suspense

A story should have plenty of twists, turns and complications that leave the listener uncertain but curious about what happens next or whether the story is nearing its end; this is the element of surprise which listeners enjoy so much.

The three "U's" should be borne in mind:

1. **Unexpectedness**

Events happened when the listener least expects it.

2. **Uncertainty**

Plausible doubt is raised as to whether the hero will be succeed in his endeavours.

3. **Unpredictability**

The listener is unable to foresee what will happen next or how the story will end.

Another effective technique is to leave a trail of clues that the listener will be able to piece together. This builds up a tense feeling of anticipation that is created by unexplained events. The technique of dropping hints and clues about what is about to unfold is called "foreshadowing".

There are many ways in which you can foreshadow; for example-

(a) **By way of (indirect) dialogue**
   The landlady handed the keys over to the tenant with trembling hands. In a tremulous voice and an inscrutable look she said to him, "You have the freedom of any room in the house, but for the one behind the red door."

   "I help you out and you help me out!" the owner of the restaurant I was working in blurted out while putting one hairy arm over my shoulder. With a feeling of apprehension I was reminded of the offer in the 'Godfather' that could not be refused."

(b) **By way of symbols or signage**
   As he was playing with the broken door-bell, the boy noticed the warning hastily scribbled on a faded sign in one window of the derelict house: "Enter at your own risk!"

   Sam was an experienced expedition leader and knew that wolves rarely howl so madly or for so long in one night. Something was inciting them. "This is eerie," Sam told guests, "I've never heard anything like it before."

   "The legend I had glimpsed on her tattoo was just like one I had seen many years before on a Chinese criminal in Hong Kong, but I could not recall what it meant, if indeed I had ever known."

This also includes prophecies (*e.g.* psychic readings, horoscopes, Mayan predictions, hermit's words) and omens of various kinds.

(c) **By way of action or behaviour**
This could be anything from a person's behaviour, mannerisms, body language, demeanour and voice tone, either whilst on their own or when other people are around. (See also the section below titled, "Show don't tell".)

(d) **By way of thought or internal dialogue**
This can be conveyed by expression of feelings of worry or self-doubt, thoughts that embody opinions, mulling over suspicions, *etc*.

(e) **By way of description**
Here you can use objects, situations/settings, the environment/scenery and changes in the weather to help you plant clues.
The heroine conceals a gun in her handbag every time she steps out of the house. Or upon returning home from his daily jog, although the house was tidy just as he had left it, he soon discovered that his laptop had disappeared!

A classic instance of foreshadowing about the big bad wolf is found in "Little Red Riding Hood":

"Remember, go straight to Grandma's house," her mother cautioned. "Don't dawdle along the way and please don't talk to strangers! The woods are dangerous."

"Don't worry, Mummy," said Little Red Riding Hood, "I'll be careful."

You should never reveal all of your "cards" at once but always have the listener intrigued to learn more.

Open loops

An open loop typically takes the form of an unanswered question or an incomplete story line. It may be advisable with some stories to leave a few unanswered questions, as this will create, in the listener's mind the mystery to get her asking you questions to complete the loop. This is especially effective as an oral story telling technique.

For an example of a story with unanswered questions, consider:

> "I was invited to this party at my friends' country house last weekend. I took Sarah along as she had just come home from a Milan fashion shoot. There were over 300 guests at the event and a special concert was heard at the end."

Unanswered questions:

- Who was the party given for?

- Where? In which part of the country?

- Who is Sarah?

- Is Sarah a model (or the photographer)?

- What kind of concert was it? Who were the musicians?

You can answer these questions towards the end of the story or just wait until the listener asks you questions about it, and you will be able to create new threads/tangents from each of the answers.

Demonstrate high value (a.k.a. DHV)

You will have only a limited window of opportunity in which to put your personality across when you meet a person for the first time. You need to demonstrate that you have respectable or desirable qualities/traits. Yet you need to take care how you say things lest excessive use of DHVs impresses the other as bragging/boasting.

When telling stories, you need to avoid featuring your own qualities and just let them be a by-product of the story itself; otherwise, people will conclude (not without reason) that you are telling the story for the purposes of showing-off.

Thus, you must merely allude to facts about yourself, without making them the point of the story. For example:

- not just you but also your ex-girlfriend were involved in an adventure,

- you travel across Europe every month as part of your job or business,

- you get invited to parties where you meet cool people.

There are several ways you can tell other people about your better traits and qualities:

(a) By having specific stories that indirectly convey the characteristics/traits you want them to know about you, *e.g.* dominant, confident, adventurous, risk taking, independent, non-judgemental.

(b) By showing them photos taken of you and then telling them a story about the occasion for the pictures.

As long as you don't explicitly call attention to yourself, you can tell people things that make you stand out from others, without coming across as bragging. For example, you can tell stories that:

(a) you lead a healthy life style and look after yourself, *e.g.* exercise, diet, nutrition, gym membership,

(b) demonstrate how you are a good listener and are present in the moment, and

(c) indirectly reveal you have "soft qualities" like compassion.

Ending

The end of the story marks the completion point and has two main purposes:

(a) to resolve the conflict, and

(b) to tie up all "loose ends" *i.e.* unanswered questions.

This is also sometimes called "the denouement".

Moral of the story

Famous stories contain practical lessons that the authors want us to learn from. This distils the essence of the story and its message in a single concluding one-liner. The "moral" of a story is the lesson learned, *e.g.* from Aesop's fables.

Aesop is the renowned Greek philosopher who wrote stories featuring animals with human characteristics, which contained simple messages anyone can learn from.

In the fable of "The ant and the grasshopper", we hear of the merry improvident grasshopper who fiddles all summer, while watching an ant working hard to gather food for the winter. The ant admonishes the grasshopper to do likewise, but the grasshopper teases the ant for worrying too much and working too hard, as food is still plentiful. But winter comes, and the grasshopper gets hungry and goes begging to the ant for sustenance, but the ant only has enough for himself and tells the grasshopper that he should have heeded his warning.

The moral of the story is – don't be lazy; prepare today for the needs of tomorrow.

We have all heard life stories from our parents and grand-parents that conveyed the message they wished us to heed so that we might grow up into responsible happy adults. These folklorish stories are usually short and based around generic themes; for example:

- helping others
  e.g. baby-sitting for a friend,

- good behaviour
  e.g. respect for elders,

- being careful about what you say
  e.g. telling the truth,

- being positive, and

- being humble.

By the same token, if we are going to tell other people our life stories, we have to make the moral personal and specific too.

Typically, it will chronicle a change in ourselves, from the start of the story through to the present time; for example:

"I surround myself with friends who are positive and helpful."

"I have learned the hard way that there are few people you can trust."

"The main lesson I learnt is that it pays to remain optimistic at all times."

"I should not try to please everyone."

"I have more respect for my elders now than I ever did before."

Story telling

Story telling is a skill that requires lots of practice and a stock of good stories to start with. Unless you are a master story teller, you need to keep the length of your stories short; typically 2 to 3 minutes of talk time at most.

The key action points that you need to incorporate into your telling are to:

(a) **Be expressive**

This includes, facial expressions, gestures, voice tone, impersonations.

(b) **"Show, don't tell"**

You have to describe the details in such a way that the listener feels as if he was in the scene with the characters (see the section titled "Show, don't tell" below).

(c) **"Check-ins"**

From time-to-time you need to check-in on the listener to see if he is following your story and do something to hold his attention and keep it from wandering. This can be as simple as nodding or asking a stock question like, "You follow?"

(d) **Pace yourself and pause at pivotal moments in the narrative**

These action points are important for story delivery. By using them, you give the listener just enough time to think and react to the story events, while heightening the sense of anticipation.

(e) **Focus on one point about the story at a time**
i.e. "zoom-in"

You must be focused on conveying your message to the listener as simply and clearly as possible. Listeners can only concentrate on one or two points at a time; thus get rid of all unnecessary details.

For example, if you are describing a holiday, talk about the most striking or memorable aspects only. For example, this could be scenic location or even a monument.

(f) **Encourage participation**

The best time to ask for audience participation is at the end of the story. You might ask questions like, for example:

"Has this ever happened to you?"

"Would you have done the same thing, if it had been you?"

"What are your views on the way she did that?

Short story – checklist

The stories you tell others about yourself will usually be short: just a few minutes in length. You will have only a limited amount of time to captivate their attention. Your story must be content rich (*i.e.* with description and detail) and your delivery must be comparably effective. You need a reason for telling the story, and it should end with a punch line or message.

You will of course be the main character, but there should be not more than one or two sub-characters. The storyline (or plot) should be simple and without sub-plots. Your story should give your audience a "snap-shot" of your life.

These are the questions we should consider telling or writing a short story:

1. **Overall**
   Is the story interesting? Is it creative?

   Does it contain a range of emotions and feelings to entertain the listener?

   Does it use imagery
   e.g. similes, metaphors, symbols?

   Have you thought carefully about the setting or background?

2. **Characters**
   Are you the main character?

   Is the story mainly about yourself?

   Do you describe your inner-self
   i.e. motivations, wants, conflicts, vulnerabilities?

Are any sub-characters necessary, and do they contribute to the story that is about you?

3. **Story line**

Does the story narrate a significant or important incident in your life?

Does it sound realistic or plausible?

Does the story line tell the listener something about yourself?

Is there a beginning, middle, climax, and ending?

4. **Ending**

Is the ending a memorable one?

Does it have a message or moral?

Have you left any open loops?

5. **Review**

Have you told this story to your family or friends?

Have you reconceived or rewritten your story in view of their feedback?

Have you noticed anything in the story that you do not like and are thinking of changing?

Exercises

Write brief stories on each of the topics below, using the concepts described above:

1. The night over a weekend, when you and your friends did not sleep.

2. A romantic email you wanted to send to a girl you like in the office, but it ended up going to the wrong recipient.

3. The strangest dream you ever had and its interpretation.

4. The holiday of a lifetime and the most memorable moments for you.

5. The reason why you jilted the first love of your life.

6. Describe the strangest person you ever met and include details of his looks, gestures and words.

7. The time you had to take in your neighbours' pet, as they went off on a fortnight's holiday.

8. The time you took up the challenge to learn French, and the adventures you had trying to speak the language in Paris.

9. How you felt and what happened when your girlfriend took you to her parents' home for the first time.

10. One of your new year's resolutions and how you went about achieving it (or not).

2. Humour

Humour in the form of comedy, laughter and jokes are all around us. We see and hear this on the telly, cinema, shows and with family and friends.

Your aim is simply to be a fun person to be around. You should let yourself have a humorous side that is able to make fun of yourself and the world, and joke around with people in your own social *milieu*. You need not go searching for humour, as it is all around us, and you need not "aim for the stars" and try to come off as the sort of "cocky and funny" person whom people would identify as being a professional stand-up comic or performer.

It is advisable to let an element of self-amusement enter into your story and joke telling. It is better not to be seeking any particular reaction from others as a result of your humour. Humour is just part of our identity and personality.

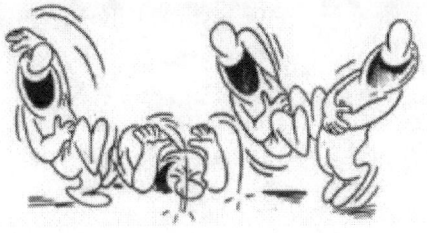

Women's sense of humour

We see girls and women giggling all the time!

Women say that the most important thing they look for in a man is their personality and sense of humour. It does not take much to get women laughing. The important point to remember is that their sense of humour is emotionally and not necessarily logical based. So, men may not laugh at the same things women find funny. Also remember that women tend to be as interested in the person who tells the joke, and pay more attention to how it is delivered than men, who are more focused on the content. This means that if they like you, they will more likely laugh at the things you say even if they are not all that funny.

The language you use to tell jokes and stories to women should be evocative and imaginative. You need to paint "the picture" in their minds. Lack of descriptive details and expressiveness can lead to a joke falling flat with them. The mental pictures you create in their minds, should aim to generate emotional states.

What's in a joke?

The jokes you hear on telly or from stand-up comics have a simple three-step structure. This simple structure always works because joke writers are looking for the fun and humour in everyday things. Following this structure, all they have to do is present their idea to us in an odd light that will strike us as funny.

This so-called "SAP structure" consists of the following three-steps:

(a) **Set-up**
   This sets up the scene and gives necessary background details; it is the "serious" part of the joke.

(b) **Anticipation**
   This brings in certain assumptions that prompt expectations so as to get the listener's mind wandering in one specific, often a "wrong" direction.

(c) **Punch-line**

This is the surprise and the funny part of the joke; the unexpected or unpredictable occurs here, upending the just-laid assumptions and expectations.

This is similar to the structure of story telling where you have a beginning, a middle and an end.

Let's review this structure as applied to the "Naughty priest" joke:

A priest had his bike stolen and suspected that a member of his congregation was to blame. Seeking advice, he consulted his trusted friend, the bishop.

The bishop suggested, "Why don't you give a sermon on the Ten Commandments? When you reach 'Thou shall not steal,' look around and see who has a guilty expression. Then you'll know who the thief is." Two weeks later the bishop ran into the priest and asked whether the scheme had worked. "Yes, it did," said the priest, "but not quite in the way you envisaged."

"What do you mean?" asked the bishop, his curiosity piqued. "You see, I was going through the Ten Commandments one by one to the congregation, and when I reached 'Thou shall not commit adultery,' I remembered where I had left my bike!"

The first paragraph is the Set-up. It gives the listener essential information about the situation and in particular about the main characters. In this case one main character is the priest and the other is the bishop. It is about a plausible scenario that could occur in real life – a priest having his bicycle stolen. It is also about a dilemma, conflict or problem that needs to be resolved.

The second paragraph is the Anticipation. It tells us how the priest intends to go about solving his problem. Ideally, as here, it creates suspense as we eagerly await the resolution.

The final paragraph is the Punch-line, where the joke takes us by surprise. In this case, a stunning secret is suddenly revealed: the priest is an adulterer!

Here is a shorter "Overreaching lawyer" joke, which also follows the SAP structure:

> A man sought professional advice from a lawyer about his marriage breakup. "What are your fees?" he asked.
>
> "A hundred dollars for three questions," replied the lawyer. "That's pretty expensive, isn't it?"
>
> "Maybe," said the lawyer. "So what's your third question?"

Targets and emotions

The first thing to do in writing jokes is to select a target; in the above jokes the targets are the priest and the lawyer. This is similar to selecting your character(s) in story writing. Next is to consider the emotional connection you have with the target(s). Remember that humour is mainly about people and things we experience in everyday life, and so we usually have some connection with them. We relate easily to things we are familiar with and can connect with.

Some examples of the people and things we have a certain emotional connection to:

- love for family, friends, pets, kids,

- hostility for bankers, lawyers, civil servants,

- jealousy of successful people, people who have things we want,

- anger at people we do not like, people who do not like us, or

- powerlessness before politicians and bureaucrats.

Making fun of everyday things (a.k.a. "What if?")

To cultivate our sense of humour, we need to get into the habit of making fun of everyday people, places and things so that people will find it easier to relate to our jokes. So, think of the twists and turns you notice or can add to everyday affairs. This is called thinking up "what if?" scenarios. For example, the following scenarios:

(a) **Location based**
Walking on a busy high street and being pushed around by people in a rush.

Imagine what it would be like if each person had their own swords and shields.

What would it be like for the older folk, for kids and for short people?

Should there be two-way pedestrian streams?

Can there be a fast lane and a slow lane?

(b) **Context based**
No one could retire before they were 75 years old:

Would we all have to be wheeled to work in our wheelchairs?

Would the office become like a geriatric home?

What would be the point of getting a pension only after 75 years, if most people are not around anymore?

How might this change how youngsters planned their future and retirement?

(c) **Character based**

What if a nasty person had a good side to them?

What if your next door neighbour is on the most wanted list?

What if you pet was able to communicate to you?

What if kids were not able to learn a language until their teens?

Making fun of characters

The characters are the most important element of both jokes and stories. However, in jokes their funny characteristics are moved front and centre, while in a story they usually are not.

Let's look at some ways in which we can make characters funny:

(a) **By exaggeration**
     e.g. big ears/nose, outlandish costumes.

(b) **By comparison/contrast**
     e.g. his hug was like a grizzly bear's.

(c) **Mannerisms, habits and behaviours**
     e.g. weird walk, accents, stuttering, laziness, clumsiness.

(d) **Lack of awareness**
     e.g. the class nerd who thinks he is cool, or
     the mate who thinks he is always right, but gets things
     wrong all too often.

(e) **Flaws, weaknesses, obsessions**
     e.g. man who goes to ridiculous extremes to get the girl of
     his dreams.

(f) **Contradictions**
     e.g. the vicar who does not believe in God,
     the 99 year old man who visits a sperm bank.

(g) **Emotions and feelings**
   e.g. laughter, crying, moodiness.

(h) **Odd one out**
   e.g. weirdoes, eccentrics, freakish events.

Tricks of the trade

A number of techniques may be applied to increase the comedic value of ordinary things:

Exaggeration

This is by far the most common technique. It is usually easy to exaggerate people (like the characters shown above) as well as things, places and events.

We often hear people tell us the "is so" statement in the context of metaphor, for example:

"He is so hungry, he could eat a horse!"

"The shopping centre is so big, we could spend all weekend camped in there."

To create your own examples you have to think outside the box, for example, have

• animals talk,

• objects move, and

• people do bizarre things.

Rule of 3

> *"Friends, Romans, Countrymen. Lend me your ears."*
> **Shakespeare, *Julius Caesar***

There is a classic way of telling a joke that has been around for ages. It starts off by setting up three persons, places or things; for example, "Did you hear about the Englishman, the Irishman and the Jew?"

You establish a train of thought or pattern in the first two elements of the joke, then you introduce a third and final element, which is the surprise. This is a "special case" of a joke, and usually follows the form pattern-pattern-surprise.

The three elements are called "comic triples"; the ones you will hear of most often are:

- A Rabbi, a Priest and an Imam,

- A blonde, a brunette and a redhead, and

- An Englishman, an Irishman and a Scotsman.

To create such a joke, you first have to establish the pattern; for example:

> An Englishman an Irishman and a Scotsman were walking through a field when they came across a cow.
>
> "That's an English cow," said the Englishman.
>
> "No!" said the Irishman. "That's definitely an Irish cow."
>
> "You are both wrong," said the Scotsman. "It's clearly a Scottish cow. Look, it's got bagpipes underneath."

The pattern used here is cow–cow–weird cow.

Here is another classic, using a similar smart-smart-dumb pattern:

> "An Englishman, a Scotsman and an Irishman were due to face a firing squad.
>
> The Englishman was the first to be lined up against the wall. As the soldiers raised their rifles and took aim, he suddenly shouted 'Avalanche!' The soldiers turned round to look but by the time they realised it was a hoax, the Englishman had escaped.
>
> The Scotsman then prepared to meet his doom. Just as the soldiers were taking aim, he shouted 'Flood!' The soldiers turned round to look, and by the time they realised it was a hoax again, the Scotsman had escaped.
>
> Finally, it was the turn of the Irishman, who had been greatly impressed by his colleagues' cunning ruses and was determined to escape through a similar diversion. So, just as the soldiers were taking aim, he shouted 'Fire!'"

The rule of three is a mainstay in movie comedies (especially the early silent ones) and in cartoons; for example:

At a formal dinner party, a man shakes the hand of a first person, then a second person, finally, as he is about to shake the third person's hand, the hand comes off (as the man is an amputee).

A cartoon bear puts his paw into a first jar of honey and licks it clean, then, still hungry, he puts it into the second jar and licks it clean, finally, he attacks the third jar, but as he tries to pull his paw out, it gets stuck. Then he walks around creating havoc everywhere.

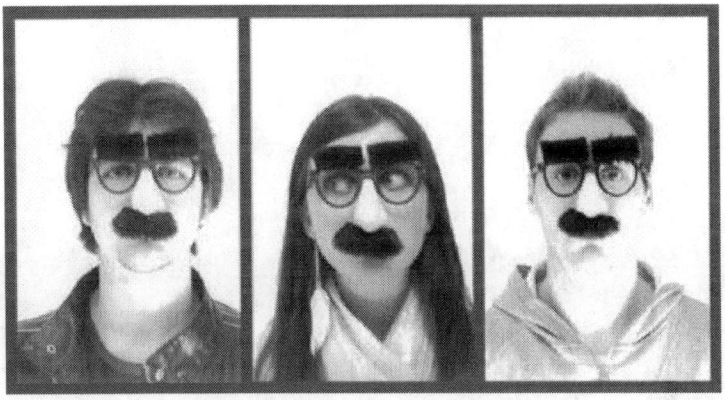

There are many variations of the rule of three. If, for example, an American were to use the technique, he could start off by saying:

> "An American, a Mexican and a Japanese walked into a bar …"

You can use this to do my variation on the "Best friends test" routine:

Here you ask a pair of girls if they are best friends. If they say yes, ask them three questions:

"Do you two use the same shampoo?"
(now they will look at each other and giggle)

"Do you two go shopping for the same clothes?"
(pause, with a smile on your face)

"Do you two have the same tastes in boyfriends?"
(the girls laugh at this point)

Situating things out of their normal context (a.k.a. "fish out of water")

This means taking things and putting them in environments where they do not belong, for example:

- carrying your fridge in your ruck sack (as you have a large appetite), or

- dogs and cats on a march demanding the same rights as humans (and debating animal cruelty).

Varying attitudes and circumstances

This is similar to the above, except it is intangible attitudes and circumstances that are situated in a wrong context.

First you determine what the normal/expected response will be, then do the opposite/reverse, for example:

- having to pay tax for being overweight,

- when taking marriage vows, the couple are required to give their divorce date.

Comparing and contrasting (a.k.a. "odd couple")

Take things that are similar or different and put them together, *e.g.*:

- a miser and a spendthrift person are room-mates,

- a pro-war and anti-war campaigner are best friends.

Spontaneous humour in the field

Now that we have a basic understanding of the theory of humour, let's review some examples that I have used before in various social situations. I like my humour to be short, snappy and above all spontaneous. Rehearsing would spoil it. We did this as kids and it comes across as harmless and natural.

All you need to do is bear in mind the possibility that you can have fun with anybody about anything. The following are specific examples of spontaneous humour that I have used with good results, and which can be used again, though it should be noted that these examples are like templates that have to be tweaked to fit your own social situations.

The spontaneous humour starts from *The premise*; this is akin to laying a foundation. You can use the same premise in varying social situations, yet each situation will have its unique stimulus that you will responds to. *The situation* encompasses everything other than what is said, *viz.* the non-verbal communication, the atmosphere, the rapport you have with each other.

Spontaneous humour may be subdivided into several categories:

Teasing

This can be anything about another person that it's possible to make fun of. Just remember that this is never about insulting or degrading people in any way; *e.g.*

The premise: The female passion for window-shopping without actually buying anything.

The situation: You are with a group of girls who are constantly talking about shopping:

"Do you girls get paid to be mystery shoppers?"

The premise: Women spending time and money on manicures and nail parlours.

The situation: A woman you are with shows off her neatly done hands by holding a wine glass.

46

"You have the most delicate 'piano fingers' I have ever seen!"

Again, do not logically analyse the meaning of the words, but be prepared to deal with her reaction.

The premise: Women being better at multi-tasking, whereas men concentrate on one thing at a time.

The situation: Your partner expecting you to do several things in one go.

"I've only got one head and two hands!"

Or, "There's only 24 hours in a day!"

You can also flip the same premise around for a different situation, *e.g.*

The situation: A girl you are talking to is constantly checking her phone for texts.

"You are easily distracted aren't you?!"

In the examples below, the premise is people's mannerisms (the way they walk, talk, think and behave): *e.g.*

The premise: "Girl-coding" or "eye talk" by which women warn each other of undesirable male attention.

The premise: Men being rowdy and competitive with each other as a result of, "testosterone poisoning",

The premise: Men having a vice-like grip handshakes as if they think they're James Bond.

Now, see if you can use these in different situations and with unique, spontaneous humorous responses.

Or:

The situation: You are speaking to a girl you like, but cannot express your feeling for her, for whatever reason.

"You are like a big baby nice and cuddly, but better behaved in front of adults."

See Chapter 7 for more examples.

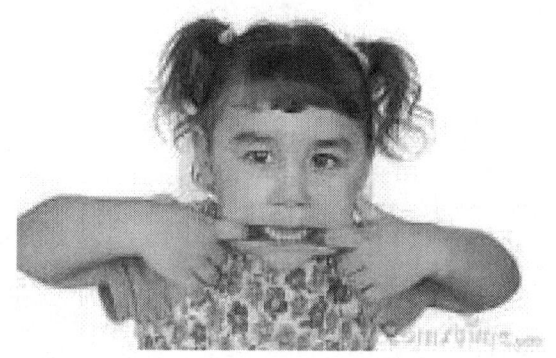

Blaming/accusing

You can mockingly blame another person for almost anything, telling them it's all their fault; this, of course, should be kept about trivial matters, lest the person misses the humour in it; *e.g.*

You're on a date sharing a big piece of cake with the girl:

"Look what you made me do – here I am pigging out ..."

There are subtler ways of mock-blaming, just bear in mind that it's your tone of voice and demeanour that must convey the effect, not so much the words:

"It is because of you I'm having to eat this ..."
(she will get the message)

Other examples:

You can say that the Internet crashed because he/she uploaded too many pictures on Facebook.

You can also "generically accuse" them; *e.g.*

"Girls from Rome are crazy …" (pregnant pause, then) "I can't believe how they eye me up in the streets every time I visit … it must be my blond hair!"

Or:

"They were following me around on their mopeds …"

This kind of humour is more memorable if you are able to give reasons for what you allege, so long as you bear in mind that humour by nature is "illogical".

Name-calling

You can call them teasing names or indeed typecast them into a role you want them to play. There is also an element of cold-reading in this (see Chapter 15 below). Give a "reason" for your accusation, but make sure it is unreal.

For example, tell them:

"You are ...

... a feminist."

... a posh girl/guy."

... a wild child (*i.e.* when they were young)."

... mummy's little girl/boy."

... a slave to fashion."

... temperamental."

... a sexual predator/player."

... an ipod/ipad/iphone addict."

... judgemental."

... a 'Sex in the City' fanatic."

Dead-pan humour (or wind-ups)

This consists of putting on a serious demeanour (a "straight face") while telling them a "tall tale" that's obviously silly. The tale must be narrated throughout in an earnest tone. You can take any topic that is not a matter of common knowledge and make a tall tale out of it; *e.g.*

The premise: Making up a story about London that sounds utterly absurd, like:

The situation: You are talking to a person who is new to London.

> "There used to be a circus at Piccadilly, but the animals were scared away by all the weirdoes, like the Japanese tourists flashing their cameras and noisy animal rights activists."

The premise: Authoritatively rating a country's culture, traditions or way of life in a way that is clearly wrong (while steering clear of making fun specifically of your interlocutor's nationality);

The situation: Telling others about my taste for fresh coconut juice and how the locals collect it in Brazil:

> "Coconuts grow on dangerously tall trees no one wants to climb, until they see the monkeys coming to get them, then there's a race to the top to see who gets there first."

Or:

> "I learned from the History Channel that the early American settlers couldn't feed their starving families, so they would roast the pet dog and stick it in a roll; hence the term, 'hot dog'."

Or:

> "I love making fresh sushi for my dinner guests, that's why I keep a fish tank at home."

Another form of dead-pan humour involves "self-deprecating": *e.g.*

Making up some "impressive" nonsense about your job, work, profession, business, invention; *e.g.*

> "I'm a vibrator engineer …"
> (then go into mock detail about what the job entails).

Making fun of your appearance; *e.g.*

> "I'm so overweight, I look pregnant."

Playing impossibly stupid; *e.g.*

The situation: If you get asked how you got to know your friend.

> "I adopted him from Africa as a baby."

52

The situation: You get asked, where are you from?

"I'm made in China!"

Misinterpretation

Here you pretend to be so clueless and out of touch, so that you interpret everything in the wrong way. This form of humour depends upon what another person has already said or done. You can "misinterpret" other people's thoughts, words, feelings and actions; *e.g.*

The premise: You know nothing about their country's culture or traditions:

"Do people eat with their feet in your country?"

Or:

"Can you imagine being French and having to eat frog legs for breakfast, lunch and dinner?"

You are hopelessly behind on pop culture and trends: *e.g.* you think that the internet is something your grandmother uses (i.e. like knitting)

Not comprehending what she says about work; *e.g.*

> "Competing in a man's world? So does that mean you're a cage fighter?"

Or:

> "Accountancy? Is that like babysitting?"

Misconstruing where he is from; *e.g.*

> "Beijing ... that's near Australia, right?"

Or, if he is black you ask him:

> "Are you from Alaska?"

Confusing the relationship; *e.g.*

Ask a pair of girls:

> "Are you two sisters?"

Watch how they look at each other and smile.

Satire

Satire pokes fun at the follies, ironies and inconsistencies of people and organisations in the mad world we live in.

In each of the examples of satire that follow, the "premise" sums up what the satire is about, while the "situation" is one particular instance of the premise.

The premise: Having a go at pet lovers.

The situation: You see people with funny-looking pets.

> "They say pet owners look just like their pets ... [pause] ... could it be they behave the same too, you think?"

The premise: Bemused by the younger generation.

The situation: You purport to explain why students these days don't learn anything at uni.

> "They spend all day pretending to "study" in Starbucks, where they can't hear themselves think."

Or:

The premise: Twitting a shopaholic woman.

The situation: You are accompanying a woman who dilly-dallies over the shoe display in a high street shop.

> "I never see you wearing but two or three other pairs of shoes besides these you're wearing right now ... what have you done with the other 50 pairs?"

The situation: You are speaking to a girl who comes across as immature.

> "You are like a big baby ..."

Or:

> "Stop throwing tantrums!"

Zaniness

You can talk about the experiences in your life in a way that appears crazy and inexplicable.

The premise: Why pets can be annoying as well as cuddly?

The situation: Talking about pets like the fighting cats in your backyard.

"One of them must be gay because he keeps yowling about his rights."

The humour in relationships,

You can make ironic or sarcastic remarks about something that nearly everyone fails at.

The premise: The difficulties of dating are legion.

The situation: You are talking to a tall girl about her dating short men.

> "You have to carry a stool for them in your back-pack, don't you?"

The premise: The battle of the sexes never ends.

Situation: You are on a date with a woman who doesn't sleep with men until after the third date.

> "Did you consult the registry of etiquette before this date or was it mum's advice?"

The premise: Women have a proclivity to dream about "living happily ever after".

The situation: You are palm reading a girl.

> "Your future is that you will settle down, get married and have 2.5 kids."

The premise: Needy nature of a person.

Situation: They say that they adore a person of the opposite sex.

> "Oh no! You would assault him ..."

The premise: You are on a date.

The situation: The other person is unsure about you and you want to reassure them.

> "You will either love me ... or love me!

Mock disbelief (or down-playing)

The premise: Women sometimes try to "Demonstrate High Value" (DHV) by talking about how goodie-goodie or (nowadays) how clever they supposedly are.

The situation: Most men would react by supplicating and agreeing with them, but you display "scepticism"; *e.g.*

> Girl: "I am studying for a PhD in microbiology at Cambridge."
>
> Guy: "No way! You're not smart enough to be a bookworm." (said with a wink)

Girl: "I work in the fashion industry and do shoots for the top labels. I am a model."

Guy: "Ho Hum! I see models popping up everywhere when I travel to London, NYC and Milan."

"My crystal ball says..."

The premise: Women have a proclivity to consult mystics and psychics. You can josh them about this by playing the role of a gypsy with a crystal ball who is going to tell her fortune.

The situation: First wait until she lets drop some information about herself; *e.g.* she tells you she will be going to the beach at the weekend –

> "Let me see ..." (act as if you are looking into a crystal ball and make a round shape with your hand) "My crystal ball says that this weekend you are going to be lying on a hot, sunny beach, waiting for Mr Right to come along and sweep you off your feet and onto a boat cruise to Hawaii."

The gypsy delivers a reading that is factual, but not evidently funny; it will be your acting skills (*i.e.* at role-playing the gypsy that) will create the humour, more than what you say.

Alternatively, you can also call on the genie in the bottle if the stakes are high:

The situation: Your friend is about to attend an interview.

> "I will rub my silver lamp and the genie within will grant your wishes!"

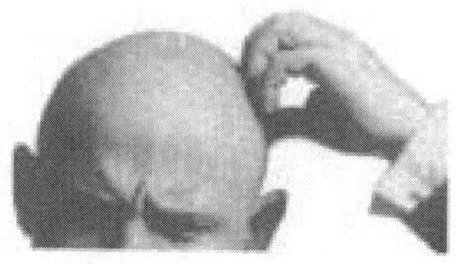

Plausible personality

While most guys will shower a woman with compliments and gifts, you will be different. Use unusual words to describe her, such as:

> "Did you know that ... you are *almost* perfect!"

> "I had to tell you that ... you are *not all that* normal."

> "I can see why I like you ... you're *a bit made of* sugar and spice!"

Absurdity/outrageousness

Talk about something that is way-out or outlandish.

The premise: The transformation of mere humans into super beings.

The situation: She is going to be late for the start of a movie.

"Surely you can put on your 'Wonder-Woman' cape and make it there in two seconds."

When dealing with a man, you can invoke Captain Invincible.

The premise: you must be from another planet.

The situation: A person gets pompous by stating something that is over the top and untrue.

"You must be living in a parallel universe where ..."

Imagine if...

The premise: If only it was easy for all of us to change.

The situation: The other person has a characteristic you want to change or you would like to see them in a certain way in the future.

"Can you imagine yourself going from...[old self] to......[new self] for at least a day!?"

Pre-emptive play

There will be times when I have not kept in touch with a friend, even if they have been trying to get in contact with me. Eventually, when we do meet up the first thing I will say, even before the friend opens his/her mouth:

"Where have you been?"

Lessons

You must use humour in social situation for your own light-hearted entertainment only.

You must avoid trying hard to be known as the funny guy/girl, or misusing humour purely in order to get a favourable reaction out of others.

Your own bemused attitude is the key to being funny.

This means do not filter or censor yourself, to meet other people's expectations.

Always let humour come out "as is", even if it's not particularly clever; your attitude of bemusement at the follies of the world will prove infectious.

Exercises

Write a humorous sketch on each of the following topics, using the information from above:

1. A tramp being invited to a royal tea party.

2. How you would find living like a dog for a day.

3. Travel guide to your local area.

4. The top thing(s) you hate and why.

5. What went wrong on your worst date ever.

6. The range of kids toys in your bedroom and how you might justify it.

7. A scheme for bilking money from gullible American tourists.

8. The pranks you and your friends got up to as kids.

9. You wake up one day thinking and acting like a robot.

10. The funniest person you know and including details of looks, gestures and words.

3. Spontaneous role-play

We have all played roles with our friends when we were young. Roles were invested with a sense of adventure, enabling us to imagine for a while we had become someone other than ourselves. Some of the roles nearly all of us have played as children are: cops and robbers, cowboys and Indians, doctors and nurses.

We can still play roles when we socialise, as we all still have that "inner child" within us, such that women played with their dolls when they were young girls, taking on the role of mothers or nurses, while boys played with toy guns.

Role-play is what actors do on stage and in the movies, where they assume the whole persona or character of another person. You can take on roles yourself, or assign roles to your friends to act out. The ability to take on roles reflects a person's self-confidence, creativity and sense of humour.

What is role-play?

The word "role-play" consists of two components that express what it essentially is and reflects its exceptional flexibility as a conversational technique:

1. *Role*

This means you and your partner assume characters such as were described in the section on story-telling. The roles need to have some "polarity" (or social distance) between them, as this will create the requisite "tension" in the relationship that will drive the story forward. It is advisable for the man to take on a dominant role; this is akin to his being the "hero" of the story.

The dominant role will lead the scenario as described below.

2. *Playing*

This implies that imagination is relied on to construct make-believe scenario(s) that you and your partner may enter into. A "scenario", however, is more of a snap-shot or single scene than a full-blown story or plot. Spontaneous role-playing is best kept short and simple: acting out a full story is too involved and in fact kills the spontaneity and the fun.

To think up an appropriate scenario you will need to decide:

(a) **Theme/topic**
    This is the most important aspect; all the other points mentioned below follow on from this one. You must ask yourself, "What scenario shall I put these two characters in?"

Let your ideas be "fluid"; *i.e.* do not think too deeply.

(b) **Location/setting**

A city, or a place like a park or a beach, or even a different time in history will do.

(c) **Feelings/mood**

It matters how you are feeling at the time, as well as how this changes over time. This should also involve emotions like love, jealousy or fear.

(d) **Dress/uniform**

This is an overlooked but important aspect that can greatly enhance the scenario: the more elaborate or unusual the dress, the better.

(e) **Drama/action**

This is created by the characters' behaviour. As mentioned above, the man will generally have to lead in order to move the scenario forward.

This shows that role-play has the same basic structure as story-telling.

Importance of role-playing

Role-playing should be fun and playful. Let's assume a scenario where the man assumes a typically dominant role. For your partner to play along comfortably, she must be convinced that you are not taking it too seriously or that you have no hidden agenda. If you are not already partners, you need to avoid over-investing early on; for example, by suggesting you and her should play a romantic couple. With that in mind, go ahead and add lots of humour and exaggeration to the script. This will make her start to feel comfortable and enjoy the role. Role-playing is important for several reasons:

(a) **It is an important attraction switch**
e.g. if you are a man it shows your ability to lead, be dominant and unpredictable.

(b) **It assumes that you and the girl have rapport**
i.e. that you and her already know each other and are in a relationship.

(c) **She feels safe**
Role-playing is just escapism, and this evokes her "inner child" of fantasy and fairy tales.

(d) **She gets to take on a role that glamorises her**
e.g. a heroine in a romance novel or movie.

(e) **Mentally at least, you rise above the crass bar/club environment**
i.e. by using your imagination you get to move to more intimate circumstances.

The bar/club environment is inhibitive for a number of reasons, among which are:

- People and their activities are stereotyped and predictable, *i.e.* you say and do the appropriate thing and she has heard it all before from other guys.
- You are already playing a role but the roles are inflexible, *viz.* you only do and say what is expected from you and her in the bar/club scene.

If your social skill level is high enough, then with spontaneous role-play you can establish rapport in minutes, not weeks.

Transitioning

You can transition yourself and your partner into your roles by saying things like:

"Let's play a game together …"

"How about if you are my new … and I am the …?"

"Are you adventurous? Let's pretend we are hopping on an airplane to …"

You can also take the last topic she was taking about and use it in your role-play. For example:

Guy: "I am from New York."

Girl: "I have always wanted to visit New York. You can be my tour guide."

Note that, you should always start the role-play with a smile on your face.

Incorporating other techniques

Spontaneous role-play is one of the most flexible of all social communication tools, especially as it lets you incorporate other techniques into the scenarios that are generally compatible with it: for example, using the "tour guide" scenario above, we can incorporate –

(a) **Push-pull**
"You would make a good tour guide, but I will need to talk to my boss first."

(b) **Cold-readings**
(see Chapter 4 below)

"I'll bet you have a good knowledge of Manhattan."

(c) **Humour**
"You get to walk my dog in Central park, in lieu of pay."

(d) **Qualification**
"Do you know the coolest bars and restaurants downtown?"

"How well do you know your way around NYC?"

(e) **Implied touching**
"Let's hold hands and dance through Time square."

"You can be my cuddly American Teddy bear."

"If you misguide me, I will tickle you."

(f) **Storytelling**
Picture romantic scenes in NYC – describing the sounds, feelings, tastes and sights.

You need to get him to participate in the adventure of the role, eliciting his choices and tastes; *e.g.* ask him:

"How would dress for the summer ball?"

"What is your favourite place to shop and why?"

(g) **Banter**
See Chapter 6 below.

Flexibility format

As noted, spontaneous role-play is one of the most flexible communication techniques you can use in social situations; it can even be "time-managed", *i.e.* projected backwards or forwards in time:

(a) **Into the present**
    This is best acted out as a "live" show:

> "You are the guest on the Jerry Springer show. I am Jerry and I give you a lie detector test with [five] questions [pretend to put electrodes on her arms]:

- Can you cook?
- Are you addicted to chocolates?
- Do you do more window shopping than actual shopping?
- Do you believe in vampires?
- Would you be scared if you were put in a haunted house alone?"

> You can use the answers you get back to find out more about her and to move the conversation forward.

As a more advanced example, use this approach only if you first establish good rapport:

> "You and I are getting married. This is the perfect place for our ceremony. Now stand up and hold my hands. I just love the music, lights and atmosphere. We walk down the aisles together while on both sides of us stand our family and friends wishing us all the best."

(b) **Into the future**

Which is often called a "future adventure projections"; it describes what the two of you intend to do later on and can also be an indication of your dreams and wishes for the future; thus if you are role-playing with the opposite sex, then choose a romantic adventure or theme, starting off as above by establishing the roles.

You can initially be indirect, then later on segue way into a something more intimate.

> "Starting tomorrow you have just been hired as my wardrobe consultant ..."

Alternatively, you can be direct:

> "Next time we meet you will be my Cinderella and we will be off to the ball with you wearing my glass slippers."

Note that the future is particularly appropriate when you want to keep the pressure off the other person; as we all know, the future is much less certain.

(c) **Into the past**

Although initially, you would have had to have described to your partner an incident you were involved in or an experience from the past; *e.g.* a holiday, a wine tasting event):

> "If only I had known back then about your skiing skills! My ski instructor wasn't that good. I wish I could have enrolled in your school as a beginner so you could be my teacher. You could hold my hands as we ski down the slopes."

Spontaneous role-play can also be –

- About you or him/her
  i.e. not necessarily about both of you at once.

- Scenario'ed by free-associating with whatever she may say (see the section titled "Working with associations" below):

  Guy: "I like cats."

  Girl: "My cats are cuddly and fluffy, but I know some feisty ones that are always scratching and fighting with each other. I will bring you over to play the peacemaker next time a cat fight erupts. Remember to bring your white flag!"

For another example, suppose you meet a person who is an environmentalist:

  Girl: "It is so important to take care of the earth."

  Guy: "We shall have to whisk you away on a magic carpet to Ecotopia, where you can get to commune with the forest till your heart's content. All the people there will be eco-warriors who recycle and never waste anything. There at last you can feel home among friends!"

Be creative with your scenarios and use your imagination. Your conversation should be about how you feel and think at the time, so avoid pressurising yourself or your partner to deliver a polished "work of art". Always remember that spontaneous role-play is supposed to be fun!

Exercises

Using what you learned above, write-up and act out scripts for role-playing the following scenarios:

1. You hire a new Personal Assistant (PA):

   Tell her why you need her as your PA, and what your standards and expectations are.

2. You take on a new body guard:

   Mention what the role entails (to protect you from all the other guys).

3. You take on the role of a teacher and she is the pupil:

   Tell her she must do as she is told, and that she deserves a good spanking for bad behaviour.

4. You are the director and she is an aspiring actress:

   Give her a role to play (preferably from a romance novel or chick flick) and direct her how to act the part.

5. You cast her in the role of a flight attendant, while you are the business class passenger who is in need of special care and attention on a long haul flight.

4. Cold-readings

In the opening scenes of The Wizard of Oz, *Dorothy runs away from her Kansas home and promptly encounters Professor Marvel, a seedy, itinerant con artist whose tacky traveling wagon advertises him as "Acclaimed by The Crown Heads of Europe", and offers his services to "Read Your Past, Present, and Future in His Crystal Ball".*

Professor Marvel, played marvelously by Frank Morgan, takes one look at the naive girl, glances down at her suitcase and says, "You're running away!"

Having missed his glance, Dorothy asks wondrously, "How did you guess?"

The Professor replies, "Now, why are you running away? No, no, don't tell me!" He looks off pensively, as if conjuring some magical power and then, as if having divined a vision, says conclusively, "They don't understand you at home!"

The wide-eyed girl smiles and says, "Why it's just like you could read what was inside me!"

The Professor then offers Dorothy a crystal ball reading and asks her to close her eyes and concentrate. As she does, the Professor quickly rummages around in her basket. He then proceeds to describe what he pretends to see in the crystal ball, referencing the items in the basket.

Whenever you make an assumption about someone you have just met and about whom you know nothing, you are "cold-reading" them. This is a technique that should be used with caution at first; you will get better at it with experience. Excess use of cold-readings and future readings in particular, may make you come across to her as her "personal-psychic".

If you already know a person, or at least something about them (*e.g.* through other friends), then you are "hot-reading" them with your assumptions. We use basic hot-reading quite often with family and friends, but without being aware that that is what we are doing; *e.g.* we might tell them:

"I know how upsetting ... must be for you."

"I can tell you are nervous about ..."

"It will not work out if you ..."

When meeting people for the first time, our usual tendency is to ask a lot of "interrogation" style questions; however, cold-reading is different: you will be making assertions about them and you will need some confidence for this.

Importance of cold-readings

Being able to cold-read people properly has several advantages:

(a) It shows that you have a good understanding of them, when most people tend to believe that other people do not understanding them.

(b) As bringing an "outsider" perspective, you may be providing people valuable insights about themselves, which they might not have considered or thought about before.

(c) You can bring out those personality traits which she would like other people to see in her, as something she wants to believe in, *e.g.* party girl, intelligent, caring, well-connected.

(d) You can reinforce her character/behaviour act, in the ways you want her to, *e.g.* independent, decisive, adventurous

> "Red haired girls are sensuous types."

> "You come across as confident and friendly."

(e) It is an attraction trigger: you are seen as intriguing as you already know things about her.

(f) You will connect with her on a deeper level than if you just ask questions. See Chapter 5 below.

Transitioning into cold-reads

You can transition to cold-reading a man/woman with statements like this:

"I have an intuition about you …"

"I have noticed something about you …"

"I get a feeling that …"

"I am beginning to think that …"

"You come across as …"

"You seem to be the type of person who …"

"Those earrings say a lot about you …"

"That tattoo is revealing …"

"I know a lot about you already …"

Observations

Your senses need to be alert and constantly absorbing the information all around you. You cannot be stuck inside your head. You will also need to develop the skills of asking questions and doing cold-readings. These are all tools that a good psychic would use when working with a client.

Observe people's styles, mannerisms, speech, behaviour, body language, backgrounds, social origins, *etc.*

You should not ask too many questions at the start or it will annoy the other person and come across like an interrogation. Once you get to know them just a bit better, they will be more accepting of personal questions.

From the things she tells you she has done (viz. travel, work, hobbies, interests, people), you can figure out and restate the values that these clues relate to.

For example:

- if she travels a lot, then she values a sense of adventure and being independent,

- if she likes cooking for guests, then you can say that she is nurturing.

Reasoning

It may sound odd if you address a series of cold-readings to a girl without giving some reasons for doing so. The questions that will likely be going through her mind may include:

- Why is he thinking this about me?

- Why is he telling me all this?

- How does he know that about me?

A cold-reading will be more believable if you can back it up; if there is tangible or visible evidence to support the cold-reading, it makes it stronger. For example, if a girl has her arms crossed and appears withdrawn, you might comment:

> "Looks like you are waiting for Mr Right."

> "Your folded arms makes me wonder if you are becoming withdrawn."

> "You must be deep in thought at the moment, because you are ignoring everyone around you."

Tricks of the trade

You need to be trying out cold-readings "in the field" as much as possible. You cannot afford to be risk-averse. Here are some methods you can use that may help:

(a) **Truisms about people**
Certain universal truths apply to all people; these are called "Barnum statements":
e.g. they have a good and a bad side; they have sub-personalities; they value freedom.

Truism about women
Certain universal truths apply to all (or most) women (see list at the end of this section):
e.g. they like to buy shoes; they prefer baths to showers; they are into romance.

(b) **Be vague/ambiguous**
Use non-specific terms that cannot be quantified/measured and have no timeframe:

e.g. most of the time, sometimes, probably, possibly, usually, likely, often, tend to.

(c) **Rainbow ruse**
If you claim that she is one thing and also the polar opposite, you are covering all the sides of her "personality spectrum": *e.g.*

> "You act like a good girl, but I can tell you also have bad girl streak in you."

> "You are extroverted in public, but you have an introverted side that people do not see."

> "Sometimes you can be full of energy, but at other times you are all quiet and reflective."

> "On the outside you are tough, but on the inside you are a softie."

There are a number of characteristics and personality traits that can plausibly be attributed to people along with their corresponding opposites:

Kind...................................Harsh

Shy ....Confident

Rigid..................................Flexible

Friendly..............................Withdrawn

Sociable..............................Solitary

Generous.............................Selfish

Happy.................................Sad

To join both parts of the statement use words like: "but" or "yet"; for example:

The first and second halves of the following statements are differentiated by:

- Time:

  "… but then there are times when …"

- Environment or context:

  "… but when you are at a party …"

- Feeling and moods:

  "… but when the sun is out again …"

- Potential and possibilities:

  "… yet you have the potential to be …"

(d) **Time line**

Cold-read the person's, past, present and future:

About the past you can read how she might have been as a school kid or when growing up.

About the future you can tell her:

- what she will be like, what her life will be like, and

- how things will get better for her.

Always stay on the positive path, and if things are going badly at present, then suggest that they will get better in the near future:

i.e. every cloud has a silver lining.

(e) **Appearance**

Tie the cold-reading to her mannerisms, to what she wears, and/or to her looks/features/expressions, *etc.*

- reading her posture and the way she speaks: *e.g.*

  "I feel you are a confident and social person."

- reading her fashion sense and clothing-image:

  "All those bangles you are wearing tell me a lot about you ..."

(f) **Fine flattery**

When complimenting women especially, it is best to steer clear of her looks and physical appearance. It is much better to talk about and praise her on the intangibles – personality, character, attitude, behaviour, *etc.*

The important things to remember are always:

- Ground your statements
  i.e. provide reasons for your cold-readings

  "You are a caring person, as you work as a nurse."

- Balance positives with a few negatives.

- Too much praise can come across as supplication; so, add in a few things that she might need to work on:

  "You are independent and decisive, but you need to learn to plan more carefully before taking risks."

- Show her that you have high standards:

  "You are the type that is punctual. This is one thing I like about you."

- Compare her to other people; in this way, you can tell her what you expect and if she needs to work harder to get you:

  "You are open-minded, but not as much as some people I've known."

  "You work harder than most people in your university course."

- Switch to another point of view; thereby, you shift the responsibility on-to other people. In other words, you are not directly complimenting her:

  "People think of you as being intelligent."

  "I'll bet your friends think that you are a kind-hearted person."

(g) Greener-grass ruse

The grass is always greener on the other side of the fence!

We tend to be always wary of opportunities that:

- we missed taking up in the past, or

- we would like to take up in the future.

In effect we are always looking for something different, more variety or the next "big thing".

A good example of this is our current job/work, in which we often feel restricted, to which we have the talent/potential for doing something different.

You can take almost any situation and find numerous shortcomings or weaknesses in it.

For example, of a successful CEO of a multinational company who spends a lot of time travelling around the world; you could say:

"He needs more stability."

"He needs to relax a bit more."

"He should spend more time with his family."

Here are some other useful examples:

To a person who has moved to the city from the country side:

"You will miss the slow pace, the calm and the freedom from crowds."

To a girl who is living with a long-term boyfriend:

"You long to meet a man who pays attention to your needs and is caring."

To a person in a mundane job:

"You might like to start your own business."

Why does cold-reading work?

At first you might be unsure if your cold-reading skills will work. Cold-readings usually work well on people because:

(a)   Especially if they are women, they are interested in the occult and unknown, *e.g.* astrology, palmistry, tarot, runes.

(b)   They like to believe positive things about themselves; in effect, you are telling them what they want to hear, *e.g.* people seek hope, they are vain, they seek validation, they believe in wishful thinking.

(c)   They accept generalities, *i.e.* even though you state truisms (about women and people), they tend to think of these as being unique to themselves and of you as being spot-on.

(d)   They will focus on things you say that are right about them, *i.e.* the "hits".

By the process of "selective reasoning", they choose to accept what they want to believe is true of themselves and to reject or not hear whatever they prefer to think is not true of themselves.

For this reason, you do not have to be true in what you say every time and can make mistakes from time to time.

(e) The discussion is about "hot topics" that are always of interest to people, *e.g.* relationships, health, happiness and wealth.

How to do it?

Cold-reading is like telling a story, except in this case it is about the listener himself. You may even be telling him things he may not be aware of. Thus, cold-reading relates to story-telling as follows:

> *A person and an observation about the person +*
> *cold-readings and a rationale = the person's "story"*

A cold-reading consists of certain assumptions, ideas, beliefs, opinions or thoughts about a person you have just met, based on observations you have just made about them.

As noted above, when doing cold-readings, it is best to back them up with rationales (or evidence if you have any). Such rationales derive from the observations you have just made. To simply make assertions about someone, without any reason, may come across as baseless flattery or insult.

A personal story is cold-reading weaved around the person.

Let's look at an example:

> *The situation*: You just met a girl who likes dancing (the person) and you learn that she has been doing it as an art form since she was 10 years old (the observation).

The cold-reading: "You are dedicated and disciplined in the things you do. You are prepared to face up to challenges, however demanding they may be."

There may be times when you may not need to give a rationale, as it may be built into the conversation, as in this example.

Up till now we have considered cold-readings in the present tense, but you can use the same techniques to cold-read the past or the future. Remember to supply rationales that pertain to the past or future.

Taking the above situation and doing a cold-reading:

(a) **About the past**

"I bet you were an ace performer in your school days. You would have always taken centre stage in school plays."

The most successful cold-reads of the person's past will be done with teasing intent (as childhood is a time of fun and play). If on the other hand the conversation has already yielded information about the person's past, then you can always cold-read them without necessarily teasing them.

(b) **About the future**

"If you keep up your dedication and hard work, you will become a successful ballerina."

Talking about a person's future is a more serious matter. Moreover, it is important to avoid positioning yourself as a fortune teller, which requires that you frame your cold-reading in contingent mode. The unpredictability of the future makes an "if" clause essential.

There are three types of cold-readings and they should be worked up to in stages as you gradually get to know the person better:

1. **Mini cold-readings**

   Start with these very small readings when you have just recently met a person. Keep them very general and vague, and do not expect a big response or reaction from them, *e.g.*:

   > "Looks like you are having lots of fun."

   > "You seem cool to me."

   > "You have a great sense of humour."

   > "You come across as innocent."

   > "You are the alpha female/boss/leader."

   > "You look like 'Sex in the City' fans."

2. **Medium cold-readings**

   As you get to know the person better, your cold-readings start to become more personal and longer:

   > "I can tell you are a person that would enjoy a relaxing massage, because ..." (give reasons)

   > "I am sure there is an adventurous side to you that I have not seen yet ..."

   > "You are the type that goes for mature and sophisticated men ..."

   > "I see that you have a short attention span. You must get bored with your boyfriends."

3. **Detailed cold-readings**

   When you have a good connection with a girl/guy and you have spent time with her/him, then your cold-readings can get quite specific:

"I'll bet you have about 30 pairs of shoes at home. Half of them you have never worn, some you wear all the time, and a few you would only put on for special occasions."

"You must have been naughty as a kid, and when you got told off by your parents you would run off and spend time on your own with your Barbie dolls."

"You have a few female friends that you can fully trust, but you decided a long time ago to get rid of the negative, energy-sucking vampires."

"You are ambitious and have dreams and aspiration in life, but you are still waiting for the right moment to fulfil them."

The general rule – called the "fork principle" – is that if you get it right, then strengthen that pathway a bit further by way of embellishment and enhancement; however, if you get it wrong, then follow the pathway as stated below. If you get too concerned about the outcome, then you become reaction-seeking and that is fatal to the communication.

What if you get it wrong?

There will be times when cold-readings fall flat, no matter how good you get at this. Maintain the air of confidence at all times and never react badly yourself to getting it wrong. If you get it wrong, the girl or guy will have a look of surprise or say that she/he is not that type; for example:

Guy: "You strike me as being a girl who likes to go out and socialise a lot" (medium cold-reading)

Girl: "Not really! I do go out but not a lot" (a "miss")

There are several things you can do in this situation:

(a) Ignore what she says and move on to another cold-reading.

(b) Tell her that she has been like that in the past or will be like that in future (statements about the future are difficult to refute).

(c) Do a "reverse" by saying the opposite:

"You have had to take a more serious look at your life and concentrate on your studies more, recently" (if she is a student).

(d) You reply back with a request for the right information:

Guy: "So you do go out a bit. What do you do at other times?" or

"Really! Tell me more about yourself."

Truisms about women

These are truisms about women in general that usually can be safely used in cold-reading; women –

* see themselves as nurturing and caring,
* are always on the lookout for a soul mate or Mr Right,
* are not interested in men who lack confidence,
* always worry/are insecure about their weight and how they look,
* want to be liked and appreciated by others,

- have a public side and a different shadow or dark side (*i.e.* sub personality),
- like to be the centre of attention,
- are driven by emotions into doing things that they rationalise later,
- think they know what they want wants from life, but are usually never satisfied,
- can put on an act or put up a façade, but the real person is behind that.

Exercises

Write up cold-readings for the following people, using the information given above:

1. A shy girl who is also conservative and reserved. You get a feeling that she opens up once she gets to know people.

2. A party girl who is a social butterfly and also has Attention Deficit Disorder (ADD).

3. A professional person who is all prim and proper but he does not appreciate your sense of humour.

4. A man who does not go out much, and you suspect does not have much of a social life.

5. A girl who is being awkward and resisting your advances.

5. Connection and rapport

We sometimes associate the word "connection" with the bonds we have with the people we know well over a long period of time, such as family and friends. A person with good "connection-skills" is able to form such bonds with people they have just met and over a short period of time. Like other social skills, we get better at this as we meet more and more people from different backgrounds.

Levels of connection

There are three "levels" of connection on which bonds can be formed when you meet and get to know people:

(a) **Small talk**

This happens when we meet and talk to people casually and probably do not expect to get closer to them. We may have reasons to keep our distance. We talk to them about trivial topics like the weather and current events.

(b) **Commonalities**

This happens where you encounter the person on a regular basis, but still do not open up to them all the way, *e.g.* colleagues at work, social acquaintances, or people who share the same hobbies or interests as you in an evening class or at a concert or event.

(e) **Deep connection**

We have a deep connection with our close family and friends. These are people we hang out with on a regular basis over long periods of time, and share with them our personal lives, thoughts, ideas, feelings and emotions.

Forming a deep connection

To build a deep connection with a person you have just met, you need to gain their trust in order to get to know them on a deep level. Once trust is established, the person will open up to you, but this will depend largely on your own social skills.

The main areas of conversation you need to focus on are:

(a) **Deep and wide rapport**

Ideally, you want to talk to him/her about a wide range of topics (wide rapport) but also establish a deep rapport on some of these topics, *viz.* her family, her past.

(b) **Fractionating**

If you dwell too much on the deep rapport, she/he will find it too intense and you will come across as a "therapist"; so, it is best to "fractionate", *i.e.* alternate talking about topics in depth, then moving on to talk about a wider range of topics. Then go back into deep rapport, but this time just a little deeper.

(c) **Which questions to ask**

Initially, you will have to ask him/her general, non-personal questions like:

> "What do you think of the city?" or
> "What are you shopping for today?"

Once you notice that he/she is willing to answer your questions, then you can make them more probing and detailed; for example:

> Girl: "I like dancing, especially salsa and street dance."

> Guy: "What is it in particular you like about salsa and street dance?"

Or:

> Girl: "I visited Miami with my best friend for a two week vacation."
>
> Guy: "Why did you choose Miami?" and
> "What was the best part of your holiday?"

For women in particular, you should ask questions that evoke emotions and feelings, *e.g.*

> "How did you feel about the experience?"
>
> "What do you find challenging/exciting about that kind of art?"

As women tend to be emotional, you will get a better response with questions like these.

Your choice of questions should be original and imaginative, because women get asked the same types of questions, time and time again:

> Girl: "I like listening to pop music."
>
> Guy: "Which pop groups do you like?" and
> "Have you been to any concerts lately?"

(these are the standard questions)

> Guy: "What is it about that kind of music that you enjoy?"
>
> "How do you think pop music compares to that of older generations?"

(these are deeper questions)

If you ask her the standard questions, then you will get an "auto-pilot" response. This will be the same response she would have given other guys who asked her these same questions before.

If you ask her deeper questions, then she will have to "dig deeper" into her thoughts and will contribute more.

Above all, remember to ask questions about extremes (*e.g.* best/worst/most memorable), as most people usually talk about the average or norms, for example:

> "What is your favourite place in this city?"

> "What was your most memorable time in Japan?"

> "What was the most exciting thing you did this week?"

(d) **How you reward and relate to him/her**
Pay attention to indications of how well you get on with a person and how many things that you have in common with and like about him/ her. Beware: you must avoid being his/her "yes man/woman" and you must avoid saying "me too" all the time, after he/she tells you about his/her likes. Having your own opinions and disagreeing with them is fine, provided you let it be known why you feel this way.

Let's look at some examples of how you can relate to her:

> Girl: "I am shy around people I have just met, but after a while I gain more confidence."

> Guy: "I am the same and I can relate to that", or "I know because I am the same way."

Reward him/her (and "relate") so that she is aware of the things you like about her; *e.g.*

Girl: "I like to ride horse back during the summer months."

Guy: "That I like about you. I like animals too, like ..."

(e) **Get to know past, present and future**
To know a person well, you need to know where they came from; where they are at the present time; and where they think they are headed.

So, you should ask questions about these three topics, while also giving them information about your past, present and future as well. Let's look at some questions you might ask:

Past

"What memories do you have of growing up in the countryside?"

"Did you like your little brother or your sister the best?"

Present

"Are you a cat or a dog person?"

"What would your best friend say about you?"

Future

This might be questions about their ambitions, aspirations, dreams, goals and desires.

(f) **The people you know**
Men too often talk about themselves using "I" statements in conversation with women. They tend to forget to tell her about their family and friends. When she goes home, she will picture you in isolation, as if a 1D image.

However, if you talk about your family and friends, she will be much likelier to see you in the round, as if a 3D image. So, do talk to her about the fun and exciting people in your life, the people you have met and your family and friends.

(g) **Telling stories**

Always give information in the form of expanded statements and stories, that are interesting to listen to.

When you ask him/her deep questions, initially he/she could give a brief or no response. In this case you need to follow the "I go first" principle – tell him/her about your own experiences first.

Give him/her something back, after he/she has replied to your connection questions. Share with her things about yourself – anecdotes/opinions/stories.

> Girl: "I like walking in nature."

> Guy: "It is nice to know somebody who enjoys their own company and nature. So many other people I meet need to have their internet, their ipods and their quick-fix routes to happiness."

(h) **Provide back-up**

One of the best ways to show him/her about your lifestyle is by carrying a camera with you. Tell stories as you explain the pictures you show him/her – anywhere between 5 and 7 pictures about your friends, family, pets, hobbies, interests and travels.

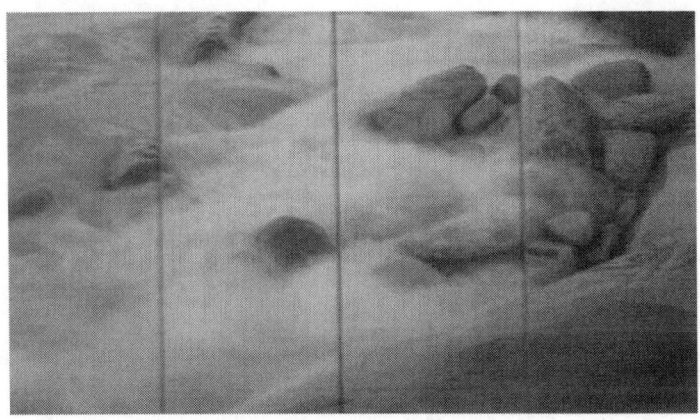

Types of stories

There are three types of stories you can tell:

1. *Connection (or social network) stories*

These are stories you tell to reveal yourself and your life. They can be surface level or deep connection stories, as a result of which, other people can get a good understanding of the type of person you are. This helps build commonalities between the two of you, which will make it easier to relate to each other.

The deep connection stories are the ones that have had a significant impact on your life and made you the person you are – the lessons you have learned, the role models you admire, and anything that has made you who are today.

Some examples of deep connection stories are:

- the decision to become a vegetarian,

- breaking up with your best friend,

- leaving home for good,

- the day I became a changed man,

- why you make the best of every day,

- what you think is the meaning of life, and

- how you got control of your life back.

2. *Grounding (or personal development) stories*

These stories relate to your ethics and your way of life, and usually feature the reasons why you are the person or character you now are. They might start with your earliest childhood memories and your past or relate your most fundamental choices in life.

Some examples of grounding stories are:

- reason for pursuing my career/vocation/business,

- why I decided to move from the city to the country,

- what I like about my long-term circle of friends, and

3. Vulnerability stories

When interacting with women, men strive (consciously or
unconsciously) to "demonstrate high value" (DHV); by for
example talking up their achievements not their failures. They
hope to impress women by projecting a perfect or superhuman
image, as if they had no human weakness. The problem is that
many women may find it hard to relate and connect with you; too
grand an image, if believed, may put you out of reach in her
mind.

You need to show her your human side by talking about your
flaws, mistakes and mishaps at least some of the time.

Revealing yourself to a woman is like the hero in a romance
novel exposing his inner-self to the reader. The main characters
in novels and soaps operas are "balanced" through showing their
strengths and weaknesses, which could be anything from
addiction to fear of flying. The hero does not hide his sensitive
side but discloses it to the heroine, which makes him seem
authentic and honest. You need to do the same by revealing more
of yourself like a confident but authentic man.

Being vulnerable does not mean disclosing to a person you have
just met, about the problems that affect your life; however you

can share with other people certain things that they may not obviously "see" in you; for example:

Girl: "You sound like a sociable person, with lots of friends and partying."

Guy: "Actually, I need my solitude. I have to have an opportunity to reflect and get calm."

To form a deeper connection with someone the vulnerability stories that you can use can be about:

- your bad memory,
- your phobias,
- your bad habits,
- the pain of an illness,
- problems of loss, and
- insecurities.

You have to get used to being comfortable with your vulnerable side and understand that everyone else is in the same boat as you.

You also need to avoid seeing women as perfect beings.

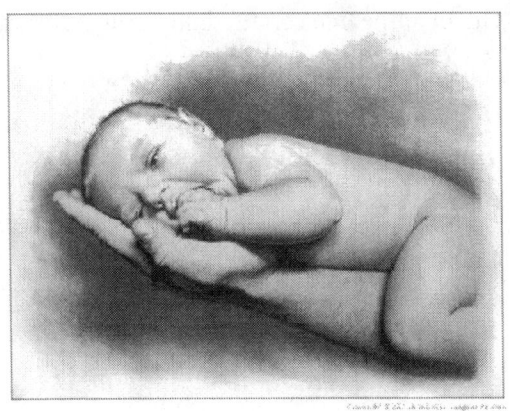

Exercises

Do and/or write up the following tasks in a "connection" context, based on what you learned above:

1. Go out and try some activity that would be new to you, *e.g.* dance class, wine tasting, fitness activity, travel, visit conferences/exhibitions; then describe the event, the experience and the people you meet.

2. Describe your hobbies and interests and why you like them.

3. Describe in detail the key people in your life.

4. How would you reply to the questions, "What do you do?" and "Where are you from?"

5. Write up a list of wide and deep rapport questions you can ask a person.

6. Write up a range of questions you could ask about a person's past, present and future.

7. Write a "grounding" story.

8. Write a "vulnerability" story.

9. Write about your identity and how it makes you unique?

10. Take a set of photos and write a story for each one.

6. Banter

Banter: "an exchange of light, playful, teasing remarks; good-natured raillery."

What is banter?

You would normally only use banter with people you know well and mutually trust, *e.g.* family, friends, girlfriends/boyfriends. However, there is more to it than meets the eye; banter also involves humour, playfulness and role-playing. It can even be seen as "busting-on" someone (in a light- hearted way) or bonding with them.

Why use banter in conversation?

It can be very effective to use banter in conversations, because:

- the attraction level is increased and the resistance shield is lowered,

- the girl/guy will think that you are a fun and playful person,

- you can create your own world or reality,

- it is spontaneous and fun in itself,

- it creates suspense and anticipation, which is resolved with laughter,

- you assume *Rapport*,
  i.e. you are not striving for or trying to force rapport,

- it moves the conversation away from tiresomely logical topics.

Role-playing

The role-playing lines mentioned above do not mean much by themselves, when read like a script.

You need to bring them alive by assuming that you are already in the relevant relationship.

One of the best ways to get into a bantering mindset is to take on roles:

Guy takes on a dominant role *vs* Girl takes on a cute role, or

Guy takes on the big brother role *vs* Girl takes on little sister role.

Expressiveness

Be expressive: vary your voice tone, make use of pauses and pacing, exaggerate and gesture.

You may not do much of this when you are with your friends; however, the person you just met in a wider social setting does not know you and your intentions, so you must get your message across by using more body language, facial expressions and voice tonality.

Early start

Set the bantering frame early on in the conversation; first impressions are all important. If you start in on bantering with a person suddenly midway through a conversation, it may come across as odd.

Within the first few minutes of striking up a conversation you should get into the mood of:

- being playful, having fun, being humorous,

- expressing emotions and feelings,

- sparing others too many questions and avoiding the trap of being tiresomely logical,

- touching, smiling, making eye-contact, and

- using banter.

At the start of a conversation with someone we have just met, it is best to use "light" banter, this is to get the other person accustomed to our playful personality; once he/she is at ease, then you can use more "targeted", zingier banter. This somewhat resembles sticking to mini (or generic) cold-reading when you have just met someone and saving detailed cold-readings for later.

"Light" banter, uses humour in the form of teasing questions: you signal to the other person that you have noted something odd in them (*e.g.* a fault, weakness or offensiveness), but you're not sure about it. Thus, you are "just curious" and seek clarity by asking them a question; for example:

"Are you high maintenance?"

"Are you girls' trouble?"

"Is that what you say to all the guys?"

"Are you always like this?"

"Hey, are you arguing with me?"

"Are you day dreaming?"
(if he/she is not paying attention or is distracted)

"You're a shy girl, aren't you?
(if he/she is not responsive)

"You're a bad girl, aren't you?"

"You guys aren't tourists, are you?"
(if he/she looks unsure about something)

These questions give the other person an opportunity to respond. You can reply back to whatever they say with another "light" banter question:

"Are you sure about that?"

"You're not lying to me, are you?"

"You are playing with me!"
(if he/she DHVs to you, then act as if you don't believe it!).

Examples of banter lines

"You girls are having way too much fun over here."

"I don't know who your boyfriend is, but he does not spank you enough."

"You are like my bratty little sister."

"You are like my little sister, lovable but annoying."

"You girls are trouble. I need to get permission from my parents before talking to you."

"I am going to put you in my pocket and take you home ... let me see if my room-mate will let me keep you ..."

"You girls are totally good girls. I will have to take you to church with me next Sunday." (girls like to be bad girls)

"You are bad; you are making me think impure thoughts."

"I want to adopt you as my Big Baby."

"You would look so cute with a Mo-hawk."

"You are cool! Do you practice being that way?"

"Are you "hitting on" me? Is this the single one?"
(if a girl/guy is making a move on you, use the second question on her/his friends in the group)

7. Teasing

Teasing is hardly a new art form, and all of us used to do it a lot as kids whilst growing up. It means making fun of ourselves, other people, and the social *milieu* around us. It does not mean you have to put people down in any way. We usually tease only our intimates, as we assume they know us well enough to have a proper tolerance threshold for our sense of humour.

When you tease someone, you show him/her the following characteristics about yourself:

(a) You assume trust with him/her,
    i.e. you need not act like strangers.

(b) You have a high level of confidence, especially as a man, as not many guys are prepared to tease a girl; you prove you do not care what she thinks of you.

(c) You show that you do not regard him/her as being perfect or "the prize".

(d) You are a fun person to be around, since you do not take things and people seriously.

(e) You come across as "childlike" – playful and unpredictable.

Teasing can take many forms and can be about many subjects, for example:

(a) **Childhood, being childish**

"Where do you hide your Barbie doll?"

(b) **She does not meet your standards**

"You need to go to charm school!"

(c) **Anything cute**

"I will adopt you as my big baby."

"You look like my cuddly teddy."

(d) **Her habits**

"Do you always do that?"

"I bet the boys run away from you when ..."

(e) **Brownie points**

"You get a brownie point for that ..."

(f) **Her accent**

"Was that in Russian?"

"That accent of yours is a bit thick."

(g) **Her mannerisms**
(*i.e.* how she sits, walks, talks and multitasks)

"Is that your sophisticated look for this evening?

"Are you the shy school-girl type?"

"You are a bit of a giggly girl."

"You sure talk a lot!"
(if she is quiet)

"Did you read that book on body language?"
(if his/her body language is "closed")

"Don't do that! It makes you look unfriendly!"
(if he/she has crossed her arms)

(h) **Relationships**

"You can be my girlfriend, for the next five minutes."

"Only good girls get to talk to me."

(i) **Comparison**

"You remind me of my bratty little sister."

(j) **Shoes, clothes, jewellery, make-up, hair, piercings, etc. tattoos**

"Those are killer heels! How many men do you have on your assassin list tonight?"

"I need to stay away from you! Do you belong to one of those girlie gangs?"

(k) **Her handbag**

"It's the size of my fridge! How many beers do you keep in there?"

"How many minutes does it take you to find your phone in there?"

"It must come in handy as a lethal weapon if you get attacked!"

(l) **Her work and profession**

"I can imagine you bossing your boss around."

"You're probably good at telling off little kids when no one is looking."

(m) **Interest, hobbies, likes, dislikes**

"I didn't know you were a hard core fan of ..."

"You must be spending all you time in the Mac shop."

(n) **Pet names or nick names**
(*e.g.* Rosie, Pinky, Cutie, Buttercup, anything silly)

"You are a pussy!"

"Do you bite?"

"You look like/remind me of that cartoon character ..."

(o) **Tell her off or calling her out**

"Where is your Fun switch?"

"Do you have an off-button?"

"Wait your turn!"

"I have eaten girls like you for breakfast."

"Don't let me come down there!"

"I can wrap you around my little finger."

"If you behave like a little girl, then I'll treat you as one."

(p) **Ambiguity or confusion**

"You will be my Ms Perfect or a good housewife."

"I cannot tell if I love you or hate you."

(q) **Implication or indirection**

"I have to be careful of naughty girls!"

"I like to tease a certain type of bad girl."

You can even tease a girl bodily by:

- pulling her hair gently, poking her in her side with your finger, tickling her, pillow-fighting,

- sticking your tongue out, making funny faces, massaging, shaking hands.

For the teasing to be effective you have to back it up by being expressive, smiling, gesturing and varying your voice tone.

Avoid teasing people, especially women, on the following sensitive topics:

- age,

- religion,

- IQ,

- family, friends, boyfriends,

- her insecurities,

- anything sarcastic and ridiculing, and

- her physical body, *e.g.* weight.

8. Questions and statements

You get to know people by asking them questions and making conversation.

In the initial stages of the interaction, you may have to do most of the talking and that will add to your value. Avoid asking too many questions at this point, as the other person does not know you well enough and it may come across as an "interrogation".

Once you get to know the person just a bit better and he/she is comfortable in your presence, then you can ask deeper questions; however, you will still need to keep your questions to a minimum. It would be better to get him/her to ask you questions too, as this will increase his/her "investment" in the conversation. (See Chapter 9.)

If you are a man, you need to avoid the generic questions that women hear all the time from men:

> "Which is the best bar in the area?" "What is the time?" "Are you a model?"

Also, avoid asking "close-ended" questions that call for nothing more than a one word yes-or-no answer, *e.g.*

> "Are you well?" "How is it going?" "Do you come here often?"

Remember from your younger days that the "five W's and H" are your friends:

> What? When? Where? Why? Who? and How?

Questions to ask

Remember that only good questions result in good answers. Questions have to be crafted carefully so as to show the listener that you understand where he/she is coming from and are able to relate to him/her. When in doubt, always start off with small, simple questions – this is good communication.

Good questions to start with usually fall into these categories:

(a) **Logistics**

"How do you guys know each other?"

"When is a good time to call?"

(b) **Connection**

"What games did you like playing as a kid?"

"Where did you go for your last holiday?"

(c) **Humour**

"Who let you girls in here?"

"Who is the alpha female of the group?"

(d) **Searching**

(Here you would get the other person to use their imagination.)

"What would be your ideal vacation?"

"What would your ideal friend/partner be like?"

"What was the most exciting thing you did there?"

(e) **Suspicions**

"Are you a bad girl?"

"Can you be trusted?"

(f) **Opinion**

(This is where you get them to reveal their beliefs.)

"What do you think about ...?"

"Who do you think is better?"

(g) **Advice**

"What would you do ...?"

(h) **Hook**

"Why are women jealous of each other?"

"Why are French women so forward?"

"Is it true what they say about German men?"

(i) **Hypothetical**

(Questions that begin with an "if".)

"If you could be an animal in your next life, what would you be?"

"If you could cook dinner for anyone, who would you invite?"

"If you had all the money in the world, how would you spend it?"

(j) **Posing choices/options**

(By simplifying his/her thinking process by breaking it into parts, this gets him/her to be specific.)

"Where do you prefer to live, in the city or the countryside?"

"Whom do you prefer, Dickens or Shakespeare?"

"Which is your favourite cuisine, Italian, French or Spanish?"

(k) **Seeking clarification**

"Does that mean you moved to NYC just to party?"

"Why did you become a vegan?"

"What do you mean by that?"

(l) **Asking for specifics**

"Can you give me an example?"

(m) **Arguing/refuting**

"What evidence do you have to support that?

(o) **Making assumptions/assertions**

(This is like a cold-reading.)

"You're a party girl, aren't you?"

(p) **Conceptual**

What do you think are the building blocks of a good relationship?

Changing questions into assertions

Instead of asking lots of questions, you can take a question and convert it into an assertion (like a mini cold-reading):

"Are you from around here?"	converts into the assertion	"You guys are local."
"What do you do for a living?"	converts into the assertion	"You come across like a lawyer."
		"You look like an academic."
		"I'll bet you do a creative job."
What country are you from?	converts into the assertion	"You look Italian."
		"You have a cute French accent."

When making assertions, give as much information as possible from the start. This will provide him/her lots of hooks, so that they are likelier to ask about you in return. Then, always give "expanded" statements as answers to the questions he/she asks you; in other words, avoid giving one-word or too short replies – give him/her more than they asked for in your reply (but not so much as to become tiresome).

For example:

1. Avoid short, generic assertions like, "That is a nice dress you are wearing."; instead give more details as to why you like her dress and point to specific things about it.

2. If she asks you "How was your day?" or "How are you doing?", avoid one-word answers like "Good!" or "Great!"; instead tell her how you feel and about your journey through the day.

3. If you get asked "What is your favourite flower?", avoid giving a one word cliché answer like "Rose". Instead seek to widen your response and give back more than what was asked for; *e.g.*:

> "I just love flowers, especially during the summer months. In my back garden............."

All of the questions in (a) to (o) above can be converted into assertions.

Our Conversation Rules

Good Listening	Look at the person talking
Take turns talking	Stay on topic Talk about the same things
Talk about good topics	No rude or mean talking
Don't talk about weight or personal things	Ask good questions

Maybe I need to review my conversation rules?

9. Open loops and baited hooks

Whenever we leave a topic, thread or thought incomplete and move on to a new one, it is called an "open loop". We do this all the time in the company of friends and others when telling them stories, narratives and anecdotes. The listeners may seek closure or resolution by trying to put us back onto the track of the open loop.

The concept of open loops is of course the mainstay of television soap operas: by the end of an episode multiple open loops have been left open on purpose. The audience is so keen to find out what happens next that they make a point of watching the next episode. Open loops create suspense and cause the audience to anticipate storyline or plot.

Here are some examples of open loops –

(a) **Questions**

This can be used with anything you observe about him/her: dress, jewellery, colour of eyes, where she is from, anything she does or says or about hobbies or interests.

"You know what they say about girls with tiger tattoos ...?"

"Is it true what they say about girls from Sweden ...?"

"Why are German girls so ...?"

(b) **The rule of three**
Give them the details of two things out of three.

Guy: "There are three things I like about you – your sense of humour and your singing ability ..."

Girl: "What about the third?"

Or:

Guy: "You have passed two out of my three best friends test ..."

Or:

Guy: "I give you two brownie points, but the third I reserve for special people ..."

(c) **As a hook**
(see the section below)

"That reminds me of the time me and my friends were in Miami."

"You remind me of my good friend Sarah."

"It's just like when I was living in the country as a kid."

(d) **As a leaving gambit**

"That line on you hand is special and tells a lot about you. Oh sorry, I forgot I have to meet my friends now ..."

"I'm afraid I've run out of time to tell you all the results of the Strawberry Fields personality test ..."

(e) **In the form of a story**
N.B. you can leave several open loops when telling a story – in the middle and especially at the end:

"I was stuck in this traffic jam for two hour in the middle of the desert ..."

(f) **When asked stock questions**
Especially by not giving the "direct" answer he/she expects or usually gets from others:

Girl: "What do you do for a living?"

Guy: "I connect people up from different sides of the world."

Girl: "What is your name?"

Guy: "Actually, my parents wanted to name me after their favourite rock star ..."

(g) **In "maintaining standards"**

"There is one thing I cannot stand about women ..."

"My ex-girlfriends have all had two things in common ..."

"I can't tell you the things that I am attracted to in men, because I don't know you well enough ..."

Baited hooks

A hook is a technique for exciting people's interest in what you are talking about. The hooks that you release, perks up their curiosity and interest so that that they want to know more.

Hooks "bait" the listener into asking you "Exactly what do you mean?" Your crafty "hook" statement results in a "curiosity" question from the listener. For this reason you need to pause after delivering the hook. Then you slowly "reel" the other person in by revealing only gradually the details of what you had in in mind. You can even jump onto another topic after the pause, so that he/she will chase you even more.

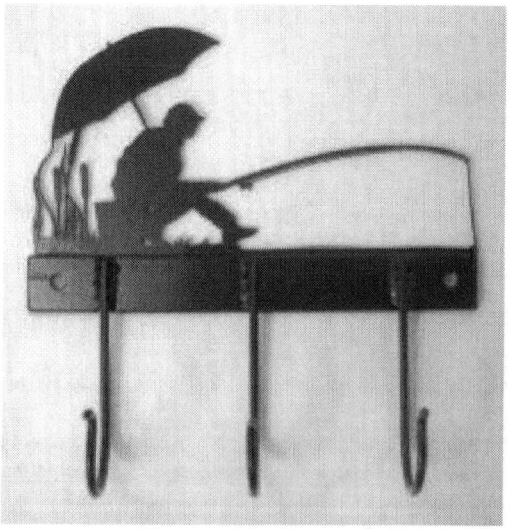

Hooks can take the following forms:

(a) **Attraction hooks**

"I noticed something interesting about you."

"You remind me of Rebecca."

"I have an intuition about you."

"There is something mystical about you."

(b) **Compliance hooks**

Hold her hands so that this hook can lead on to your reading her palms:

"Your hands are amazing."

"You have unusual hands."

"Your hands say a lot about you as a person."

(c) **Rapport hooks**

If he/she asks you the stock questions about yourself – What is your name? Where are you from? What do you do for a living? Do you do for hobbies/interests? You can reply:

"Have a wild guess!"

"You wouldn't believe it if I told you."

"It's something fun and exciting."

"I come from a distant and exotic land."

"I get up to some dodgy things in my spare time."

(d) **Story hooks**

There are a number of ways of leaving hooks in stories that will make them exciting and increase anticipation and tension.

"We were invited to this party on a paradise island ..."

"There was something spooky about the house ..."

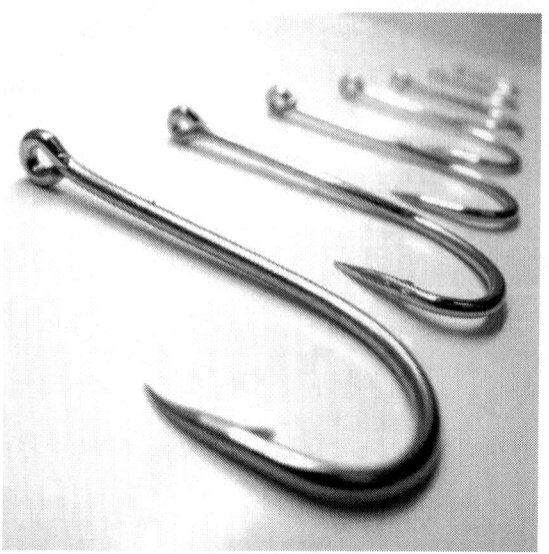

After the open loop, the listener will think to himself, "What happened next?"

The baited hook is a special type of an open loop, in that it is intended to create a feverish sense of anticipation.

N.B. This is not the same hook as the one described in story telling, because this baited hook does not grab the listeners attention at the beginning of the story.

10. Multiple threads

(*a.k.a.* multiple topics, multiple tangents)

The Fates (Moirai) in Greek Mythology

In Greek myth, the three Goddesses of fate, metaphorically write the story of each of our lives from birth to death. The three sisters were said to sit beneath the earth and weave our destinies.

At the birth of each person they appeared spinning, measuring, and cutting the thread of life, as below:

- **Clotho** (the spinner) depicted with a spindle, spins the thread of destiny and decides on the arrival time of each individuals birth.

- **Lachesis** (the measurer) depicted with a scroll or globe, has the role of measuring the length of each thread in life.

- **Atropos** (the cutter) depicted with a pair of scales or shear, has the fateful role of cutting the cord of life bringing each individuals destiny to an end.

Now, more than 2,000 years on, we still use the above ideas in storytelling, like that of spinning or weaving a story. All stories have a beginning (birth), a middle (life) and an end (death). A story can be seen as a thread and our conversations consists of multiple threads.

A conversation with persons we know typically contains several conversation threads at once; these threads are either

1. **Old**
   i.e. pertaining to the topic already started,

or

2. **New**
   i.e. pertaining to a new topics that we have just brought up.

We all have a tendency to cut old threads off because they do not serve our purpose at the moment or because they have led nowhere. We begin new threads in order to talk about new experiences or new ideas we have recently been through.

So, when you are in rapport with friends, the key points to remember about threads is to:

(a) Use multiple threads,
   i.e. you have several threads open and on-the-go at the same time.
   This will stop you from running out of things to say and make your conversation varied and interesting.

(b) Switch back and forth between threads seamlessly, without finishing the previous thread,
   e.g. you start by talking about where you plan to go out tonight, then you move on to talking about the weather or your car.

(c) Leave some threads open by the end of a conversation,

i.e. you won't get back to these threads to close them until you meet the other person again; this is an "open loop".

(d) Ensure that each thread has a "relatedness",
that prevents it from stagnating – see the next section on "Linear logic and endless loops"
i.e. avoid clichéd answers and hackneyed platitudes.

(e) Give all of the threads of your conversation emotional content.

If you are meeting someone for the first time, it is important to have several "directional" threads ready to go, right from the start; this puts the conversation into "rapport phase", as if we already knew these people as friends. *Remember*: whenever you leave a thread "open" or incomplete and move onto a new one, the old thread is called an "open loop".

Linear logic and endless loops

Think of your conversation as a dance rather than a walk!

Much of our conversation is logical and/or factual in nature, in the course of which we impart and interpret information. This type of conversation occurs in the business world all the time; however, in a social setting, if we get caught up in too much of this, we can end up going in circles; we get "stuck" on the same topic.

Take, for example, a conversation between two men in a bar after work:

Man 1: "How was your day today?"

Man 2: "Alright."

Man 1: "What do you do for a living?"

Man 2: "I work in IT."

Man 1: "What does it involve?"

Man 2: "Mainly working on projects."

Man 1: "Do you work long hours?"

Man 2: "Most of the time."

Man 1: "What do you like about your work?"

Man 2: "The pay is good."

Man 1: "How about the people you work with?"

Man 2: "They are cool."

As you can see, this conversation is about Man 2's work and it is factual and linear in nature. If the conversation continues in this way it will soon fizzle out. It is trapped in a "loop" about work and the longer it stays there, the harder it will be to get out of this loop and to move on to other topics.

Working with associations

To get away from this linear mode we can use "associations" or associated topics (or threads) in our conversation. Say for example we are talking to our friends about travel: there are other topics that are associated with travel (as listed below).

Using a multiple threads approach, you can start a conversation with, say, five main topics that you like talking about, one of which might be travel; then you can switch seamlessly between this and its associated topics. This means that from one main topic you can branch out into several associated topics.

Main topic – travel

Associated topics: Cuisine, People, Culture, Tradition, History, Adventures, Experiences, Weather, Business.

Returning now to the conversation between Man 1 and Man 2 above, what are some of the topics you might associate with "work"?

Main topic – work

Associated topics: Travel, Hotels, Colleagues, Conferences.

Continuing their conversation, let's see how we can use association to transition to other topics:

Man 1: "How was your day today?"

Man 2: "Alright."

Man 1: "What do you do for a living?"

Man 2: "I work in IT."

Man 1: "What does it involve?"

Man 2: "Mainly working on projects."

Man 1: "Do you work long hours?"

At this point Man 2 decides he does not want to talk about work anymore and changes topics:

Man 2: "Most of the time, but I'll soon be going on a holiday for a couple of weeks. It will be my first visit to Cuba, and I am looking forward to it. Have you ever travelled to any exotic lands?"

Man 1: "I've been to several Asian countries and to China many times."

The conversation has moved away from work and now is about travel. From here on, you could also use any of the topics associated with travel, to broaden the conversation and keep it from stagnating.

Multiple threads – checklist

Here is a checklist for how you can use multiple threads to keep the conversation flowing:

(a)   Start a conversation or transition into a new topic with either statements or questions:

"What do you think of the coffee here?"

"Which cocktail would you recommend?"

"This seems like a trendy venue with friendly people."

"The people in here are all smartly dressed and the place is buzzing."

(b)   Ask open-ended questions.
This is about finding out about the other person and will get them involved:

"What do you like about your laptop?"

"I would like to visit Oslo. What experiences would you recommend there?"

(c) Make open-ended statements.
This is about your contribution to the interaction and adding value to it. Drop plenty of hooks and open loops, as discussed in the section on storytelling. Always observe the people and the surroundings; this shows your social intelligence. Do not feel afraid to share your thoughts, emotions, feelings and opinions:

"You are staring intently in your book. Looks like you are really enjoying it."

"The atmosphere in this place is amazing. The music is cool and the décor is stunning."

(d) Expand on the material you are given.
Give more than you get.

Above all, you need to listen carefully to whatever the other person is saying, and make a point of relating relate to it. If you jump on to an unrelated topic, it may appear that you are ignoring them:

Other person: "I like going to dance classes in my free time."

You: "I like to go dancing as well. I have always been interested in Salsa and street dance. It is relaxing and helps you unwind after a day's work. I have made a couple of good friends at dance class. I've been attending classes for three years and I would say I am at intermediate level."

11. Looking and listening

Wherever we hang out with people, we need to be absorbing all the important bits of information around us. This information gathering enables us to create rich topics of conversation; it also distinguishes us from other people, who are usually "stuck in their heads" and aren't observing things around them.

There are three things we need to observe:

(a) **The person we are talking to**
This means observing their looks (eye colour, hair, skin), moods, feelings, emotional states and behaviour. Observe carefully what people are wearing: clothes, shoes, tattoos, hairstyle, jewellery, hand bags, accessories, make-up.

(b) **Other people**
Observe the people around you at the event and notice what state they are in.

(c) **The environment/location**
This can include the sights, sounds, colours, textures, music, food and drinks.

Observation

We can use all this information around us to enrich our conversation with another person by:

(a) **Asking him/her questions**

"Hey, that ring looks interesting! Where did you get it from?"

"Are you people watching?"

(b) **Making statements**

"That scarf looks like designer material!"

"You look bright and radiant today!"

(c) **Complimenting him/her**

"You sure look special today!"

(d) **Teasing**

"That overcoat of yours is like a cuddly bear."

"Your mind is wandering off again."

(e) **Telling stories**

"Those shoes of yours reminds me of ..."

"My best friend always used to complain about ..."

Listening

At all times during an interaction you should listen to what the other person is saying. Every bit of information they provide can be used to further the conversation.

A good listener is someone who has an interest in other people. So, pay attention at all times!

Listening without prejudging

We need to listen intently to others and with an open mind; this means learning to listen without prejudging. The usual tendency is to mentally pass judgment on anything, by thinking to ourselves:

> "This is not right."

> "This is bad."

> "He is strange."

> "She is not my type."

It is better to first listen carefully and let all your assessments, opinions and labelling fade away.

12. Complimenting and women's interests

Women tend to spend lot of their time on their appearance and on getting prepared for going out.

They do like attention and compliments, provided it is genuine and sincere and that the person giving the compliment does not have an agenda or is doing it to get favours from them.

If you are giving compliments to a girl you have just met, it is best to steer clear of complimenting her on her looks; however, you can make comments like:

"You are confident and well spoken"

Or:

"You have a good aura about you."

There are many aspects about which you can compliment women, and they include:

(a) **Fashion**
If she is impeccably well dressed you could start with a compliment about her clothes, style, jewelry, accessories, shoes, hair style, tattoos, make up or nails.

(b) **Smile**
You can say, "I just couldn't help notice that you have the most incredible smile. It lights up the whole room."

(c) **Posture**
You can say, "You carry yourself with an elegance and poise that I rarely see in a woman."

(d) **Energy and fitness**
You can say, "You have this magical energy about you that radiates positivity!"

"You must be a serious fitness fanatic or else a ballerina."

(e) **Eyes**
You can say, "You have particularly interesting, bright blue eyes."

(f) **Personality and character**
You can comment on several things here if they stand out, such as her being adventurous, fun, intelligent, friendly, knowledgeable, social, outgoing, open-minded; as well as her likes and dislikes, hobbies and interests.

Follow up your compliment with a simple question. This will avoid the awkward silence and get her talking. For example:

"You are wearing a beautiful hat. Where did you get it from?"

"That is beautiful jacket. Is it mainly for the winter?"

"I like your red lipstick and dress. Did you plan it or is it a coincidence?"

"That is an amazing necklace. What kind of stone is it?"

Here is a list of "dos" and "don'ts" when paying compliments:

Do:

(a) **Be specific**
Rather than telling her that you like her dress, let her know exactly what about it you like, with details.

(b) **Be observant**
Most men are not aware of the effort and time women spend on their appearance. You need to let her know that you have noticed and do appreciate what she has done, *e.g* a change in hairstyle.

Also, look for the things that are not always obvious.

Don't:

(a) **Compliment her on her looks**
Unless you know her well, *especially* weight, body.

(b) **Overdo it**
Avoid complimenting her too much or too often.

Women's interests

A good way to understand a woman is by looking at what interests her. Women are stereotyped as having common interests like shopping, chocolates and celebrities. It is important that you do not lump all women together with stereotypes. Always look out for what makes each one unique.

When getting to know a woman better, we have to be careful not to be too inquisitive about their individual lives. Especially be careful not to ask them too personal questions initially, such as:

"What is your bedroom like?" "What do you wear in bed?" "Have you had cosmetic surgery?"

It is good to know as much information as you can about the topics below, because it will make you will stand out from other men. At the same time, you do not want to become an expert on these topics, as you will come across as her "girl-friend".

There are several places from which we can source our information about women:

- from the women we meet socially,

- from the girl-friends we have known, and

- from media sources, such as the internet, news and books.

Without trying to stereotype, some of the main topics that interest woman are, in no particular order:

1. Shopping and fashion.

2. Relationships, including family, friends, boyfriends, babies.

3. Dining and dieting.

4. Music.

5. Movies.

6. Romance and sex.

7. Pets.

8. Celebrities.

9. Travel and adventure.

10. Romance novels and women's magazines.

11. Art – dance, photography, theatre.

12. Work/career/business.

13. Ambitions and aspirations.

14. Studies and schooling.

15. Health and fitness – gym, running, nutrition.

16. Current affairs and environment.

17. Occult/paranormal – astrology, magic, dreams, witchcraft.

18. Mind, body, soul – meditation, yoga, spirituality, massage.

19. Motivations – passions and values.

13. Description and details in stories

Do not leave the techniques of description and detail when telling stories to "Dickens the master storyteller." Instead, learn to use these actively in all your conversations!

By using vivid description and details in storytelling and writing, you will be giving the story a life of its own. You need to use description and details in each of the components that make up the story – the plot, the setting, and the characters. By doing this you are making the listener or reader feel as if they are "present" in the scenario, experiencing the events being described.

Here is a list of techniques that are integral to good, creative storytelling and writing, which will enhance your narrative skills:

(a) Compare and contrast.

(b) Highlight senses, emotions, feelings and thoughts.

(c) Narrate from different points of view.

(d) Show, don't tell.

(e) Include dialogue.

(a) Compare and contrast

Comparing and contrasting is an important part of creative writing. We compare and contrast things all the time in our daily lives without being fully aware of it. This is particularly so when it comes to making decisions like what to buy or which way to which way to go.

Before we can use comparison and contrast, we must identify things having something in common or belonging to a certain group; for example, different type of holidays, cars, houses, computers, *etc.* It is also important that we have a good understanding of both the objects under scrutiny, and that we bring out the salient points of interest; in other words, we do not want to focus on dull and mundane "common-knowledge" material. You have to interest the reader or listener, so discuss things that are not obvious.

When you compare two items you are looking for similarities, and when you contrast them you are looking for differences; for example, we can compare and/or contrast pairs of items like:

- Mac or PC.

- Oxford or Cambridge.

- Starbucks or Italian coffee shops.

Let's take an example of comparison/contrast: two animals we are all familiar with, cats *vs* dogs:

Comparisons	Contrasts	
Both most popular domestic animals	Cat keeps itself clean	Dog is rough and dirty
Both like the outdoors	Cats do not need to be cleaned	Dogs have to be bathed
Both can be aggressive	Cat is like a female	Dog is like a male
Both shed fur	Cat likes milk	Dog likes meat
Both need shelter indoors	Cat is a good pet	Dog is man's best friend
Both like care and attention	Cats do not have to be walked	Dogs have to be walked

You could compare/contrasts many more items; *e.g.* cats having nine lives, superstitions.

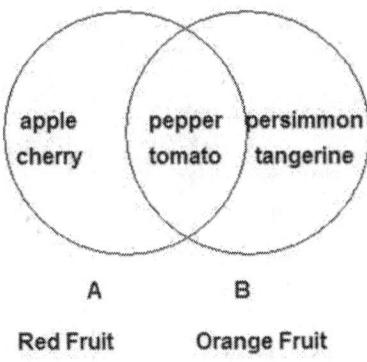

A   B

Red Fruit   Orange Fruit

Exercise

Compare and contrast the following pair:

- Going to a move or watching a movie at home.

- Living in the countryside or living in the city.

- Having a male friend or having a female friend.

- Drinking tea or drinking coffee.

- Doctors' medicines or natural remedies.

- Camping in the forest or sleeping in a hotel.

- Learning to ride a bicycle or learning to drive a car.

- Snow fall or rain fall.

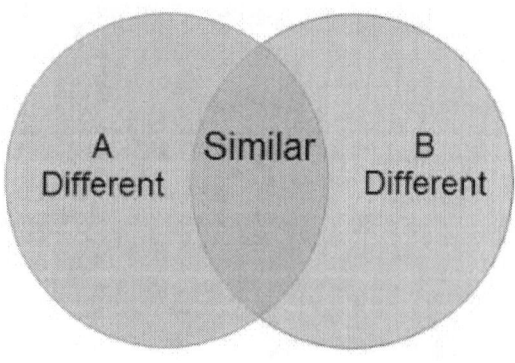

(b) Highlight senses, emotions, feelings and thoughts

A large part of storytelling is about describing, including both:

(a) **The tangible**
   i.e. our senses of sight, sound, taste, smell and touch, and

(b) **The intangible**
   i.e. our thoughts, emotions, moods, states, feelings.

Ideally, you will want to use a good mix of both.

Always be fully aware of your surroundings, and take care to describe this with each and every one of your senses. Most people when they are describing things only describe what they see.

Let's take for an example the description of a party we have been invited to, using all our senses to describe it:

1. **Sight**
   The colours of the room and its lighting, what people are wearing and how do they look, darkness and light in the rooms, room layout, people's actions and behaviour.

2. **Sounds**
   What the music was like? Noisy or quiet rooms?

3. **Taste**
   What the drinks and foods were like? What their quality and quantity was?

4. **Smells**
   Anything nice or offensive, perfume, aromas.

5. **Touch**
   Shaking hands with people, being pushed, touch other people, textures of seats or sofas, *etc.* smooth, rough, hard, soft.

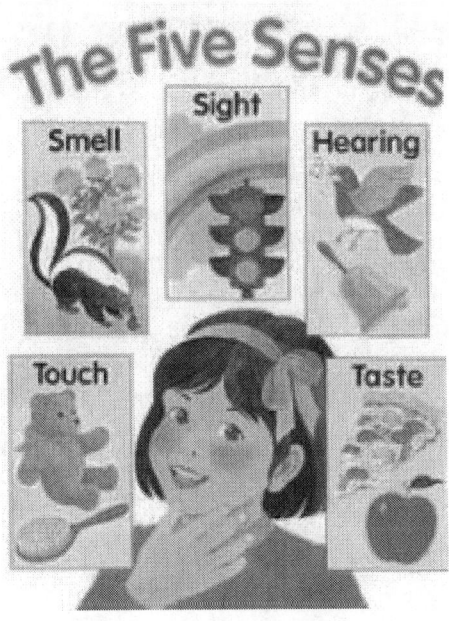

It is always a good idea when telling stories and talking to other people to reveal your inner state: emotions, feelings and thoughts. These things are not obvious to others, and you need to describe them if you want people to understand you better.

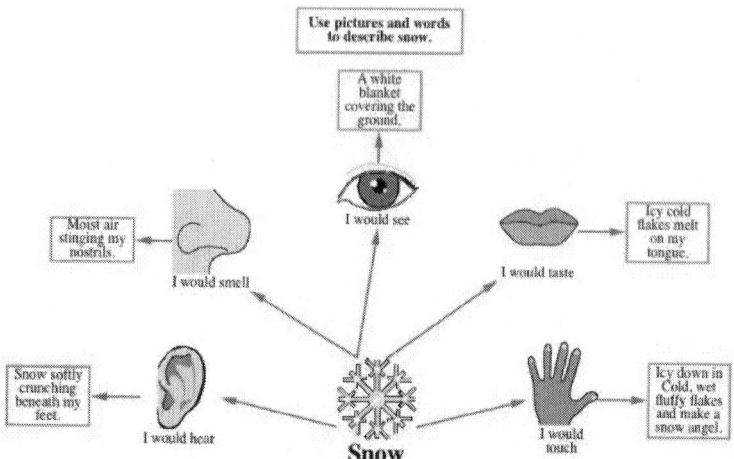

It is advisable to cover a wide range of these emotions, thoughts and feelings. Let's take the example of the party above to describe these inner states:

1. **Emotions and feelings**

    This may or may not cover the whole range from positive to negative emotions – happiness, excitement, joy or anger, jealousy, hatred. You can tell why you felt as you did at a particular event as well as how much you felt it, *e.g.* someone spilt a drink on you, you had to listen to a boring conversation, you enjoyed the dancing, *etc.*

2. **Thoughts**

    This is about all the things that we are going through your mind at the party:

What did you think about the people? Did you want to stay or leave? How did this compare with the other parties you have attended?

(c) Narrate from different points of view

Whenever we tell or write a story, we need to carefully consider from whose point of view we are telling it. In storytelling it is important to be skilful in switching between different "points of view" (POV) smoothly. Let's take the example of the party, and look at the three main POVs:

1. **The narrator**
   This is the person who is telling the story – the observer who sees everything what is going on at the event. The narrator has a bird's eye view of the party but is also able to identify and home in on significant details.

2. **The characters**
   In any story there will be a number of characters both major (hero/heroine) and minor. Each one can tell us something about what is going on in the story from their own point of view. POV makes it more personal, as each character expresses their own thoughts, emotions, words and deeds.

   Every character should have a different opinion about and reaction to the other (main) characters in the story; for example, the heroine may think that the hero is a good guy, but the cops think he is a bad lot or his acquaintance think he is greedy.

3.   **The group**

This is the POV of the group as a whole, which may give a composite opinion on events; for example, it might be said that most people were pleased with the party.

Another POV can also be used: that of inanimate objects, animals, trees, *etc.*; for example, if you say one of the guests was pouring his drink into the potted plants, you could relate that the plants got drunk that night!

(d) Show, don't tell

In any creative writing course you will constantly be told "show, don't tell". This means especially that you should avoid overusing the omniscient narrator point-of-view, and eschew preaching or teaching or any other didactic kind of narrative technique. Rather paint a vivid picture, and bring the story alive. You have to draw the listener or reader into the experience through your characters' thoughts, feelings, acts, words and sensations.

Let's take a very commonplace example – I can "tell" the listeners or readers:

> "The man was confident as he walked into the saloon."

Narrating the same event in "show" mode:

> "The man walked in with a big grin and shoulders square. He glanced about at everyone there, and saw a pretty girl behind the bar. Offering her his rough hand, he said in a softened tone, 'Howdy, my name is John Wayne.'"

Both narratives were about the same self-assured man as he was entering a saloon; however, when we tell or "lecture" the listener/reader, we leave out significant details and, in particular, we miss showing or painting a picture of John Wayne's confidence. When we "show" instead of "tell" what happened, the listener/reader can, for instance:

- Picture the swagger with which he walked into the saloon.

- Hear his suave tone of voice.

- Feel his firm handshake.

When to "tell"?

"Telling" is the mode people most often communicate through in their everyday conversations with others. People shy away from "showing", and use a minimum of description and detail.

Telling essentially consists of skimming or summarising the story; you skip description and details and state matters in the abstract. Instructors in creative writing or public speaking are constantly reminding us to "show, don't tell", yet telling does have its proper place. It bypasses the less important bits, or at least minimises them; kind of like a short-cut. Also, telling is needed to narrate events over a long span of time (*viz.* time compression), as telling takes up less time than showing.

It sets forth an abstract overview of the story or matter, using stylised facts and observations, mainly from a narrator's or reporter's point of view, in order to impart information, but not to engage the reader or listener emotionally in the human interest of a story.

The most important conversation content that is missing when you "tell", is emotional expression. By skimming over a large number of topics in a short period of time, you avoid expressing yourself; like a reporter arriving at a scene, you are in it, but not part of it.

It is common for people not to express (or expose) their emotions to other; this is particularly true of men. However, the downside of this is that, you will never be able to get the listener to be fully engaged. If you do not express your emotions in a conversation, then you are not speaking with passion (see Chapter 20).

In the saloon scene, if we do want to narrate an effective story, we must relay the concrete signs of John Wayne's social aplomb, and so we zoom in on his entrance. We can get away with omitting or merely "telling" the less significant facts of the story.

Why should you "show"?

By painting the scene and showing it to the reader or listener, you become the director of your own script, picking and choosing the significant detail to illustrate with. What you "show" in your story is something like what a movie director shows the audience on the silver screen.

As a director you have to choose carefully not only what to show, but also what not to show. Over-doing the detail can overwhelm the listener/viewer. It is best to use specific, action-oriented details to make your impressions.

"Showing" should especially be resorted to in these parts of the story:

- introducing or revealing a character,

- establishing the mood,

- building suspense,

- creating and resolving conflict and tension, and

- painting emotional and dramatic scenes.

Let's take the saloon scene further and assume that our hero John Wayne fancies Rebecca, the girl he offered his hand to. How does one avoid "telling" the listener that John Wayne likes Rebecca, but "show" it instead? You could, for example, start by saying:

> "His eyes twinkled as he smiled her way, smoothing his black hair back. He spoke softly and strove to express himself genteelly."

> "He felt the excitement rush through his body as he turned to face her."

Below are two examples of stories that involve:

(a) **Mainly telling**
    The story is "Mafia boss of NYC".

(b) **Showing and telling**
    The story is "Safari adventure".

Each story will be followed by an analysis.

Mafia boss of NYC

I was visiting NYC with a good friend of mine for a couple of weeks. We stayed at the Hilton hotel in downtown Manhattan, not far from China town and Little Italy. I love this neighbourhood and visit it several times a year on business. I have known my friend Charlie for many years, and this is the first time he accompanied me to NYC.

On one of these trips, we stayed a week and for lunch frequented this cosy little Italian restaurant, not far from my office. It was run by a charming old couple who have owned the place for over thirty years. They welcomed us and liked the fact that we were British. I would order my favourite dish of seafood spaghetti with a glass of Italian wine.

On the last day, events took an unexpected turn. I arrived at the restaurant at lunchtime with my friend and ordered the usual. After lunch, the owner asked me into a side room and told me he wanted me to do him a favour. He said in this thick Italian accent, "I will make you an offer you cannot refuse! You take this parcel back home to London with you and deliver it to my friend who will be waiting at Heathrow airport. Never open it. For this favour, I will pay you $1,000 in cash."

I took the parcel at once, which was the size of a shoe box and heavy, and put it under my arm. Charlie was waiting for me and I explained to him what just happened. I told him I was happy to help the old man out, even if he had not paid me.

Charlie's jaw dropped and he looked at me in amazement saying, "What have you done?"

Story analysis – mainly telling
This is how most people, narrate or report on their travel adventures. It is a litany of facts, but devoid of description and detail, which is left entirely to the reader's/listeners' imagination.

Safari adventure

I was handed the keys to bungalow 13. We were told that the eco-friendly accommodation was located on the outskirts of the Serengeti National park in northern Tanzania.

My room was spacious and had a polished wooden floor. On two sides of the room were sliding doors leading on to a porch. During the afternoons you could laze around there and watch the animals coming out of the under bush for a bite of the fruit and leaves. We were under the forest canopy, and the noise of the birds chirping above was continual.

In the middle of the room was a huge stretched tiger skin lay on the floor, with a ferocious looking head at one end. The double bed looked clean and comfortable, except for the stuffed leopard's head hanging over the bedstead.

"Is this what they mean by eco-friendly?" I wondered to myself.

I was expecting a tranquil night as I laid my tired body to rest and curled up under the quilt to sleep. The only noise I could hear inside my room was the fan revolving above my bed. From outside, the hyenas were laughing their strange laugh in the distance, as if wishing me a good night's sleep.

Little did I know that I was sharing the accommodation with a family next door. There were stomping sounds, as if someone was trying to make a point. The noise came through the thin bamboo wall that separated our rooms.

A little boy's scream suddenly shattered the silence.

"Shut up, Johnny!" his mother kept shouting at him.

The next morning, as I watched the sunrise through the glass doors, I felt tired as if from a lack of sleep. Still, I was looking forward to the daylong safari and a proper English breakfast with freshly made Rooibos tea.

Around the well-laid buffet, I caught my first glimpse of the little boy. He wore a baseball cap back-to-front, his t-shirt was rumpled and stained, and his trainers were muddy with the laces undone. He walked with a wobble, moving forward with legs going from side to side instead of straight.

"I want chocolate now," the little boy demanded of his mother.

"You are not going to have it unless you eat your breakfast", she admonished him.

He folded his arms and sulked with a downcast head, refusing to acknowledge my presence.

After the breakfast, the Maasai guides led our group of seven to an old, rickety, open-top vehicle. They explained the things we should not do when we arrived at our destination, and that it would be a two-hour drive getting there.

The sweltering heat hit me at once; it was still early morning, yet the temperature must have already been in the mid-forties. Sweat was rolling down my face and back, which I did my best to wipe off with a handkerchief that was soaked.

Pinned to our hard seats we were driven at speed along the dusty rural track. The bumps and potholes kept tossing us into the air, to land with a thump back onto our seats. If ever we slowed to a crawl, we were immediately swarmed by mosquitos, which I had constantly to rid myself of by wriggling and slapping my arms and body. "It might spare us being baked and bitten if they were to cover the vehicle," I thought to myself.

As the vehicle swayed from side to side, the boy became irritable. He would not sit still and became increasingly restless and on edge.

"I want to go home," the boy cried as he began to wail loudly. His mother wiped his face with his t-shirt.

"We'll get there soon!" the guides shouted to us, as if they knew the journey was a painful experience for visitors.

We reached the safari staging just before noon; it was watering time for all the beasts of the wild. Animals and birds, large and small, were gathered around a watering hole. A few of the animals had taken cover from the heat by sitting under the shade of some majestic trees nearby. Our vehicle was positioned a few feet away so that we could see and film the animals. Our presence did not seem to bother them, as they were more interested in the water. Rhinos, elephants, giraffes, zebras, *etc.* had come together in harmony.

Suddenly, one of the guides motioned for silence, pointing to a lion that was passing by our vehicle and approaching the lake. We stood still with mouths agape, chests heaving with the excitement of fear. The lion seemed to have locked its eyes on the animal that was to be its prey, lying low and creeping up on it unnoticed. The other animals did not see the stalking lion.

"Where's Johnny?" his mother suddenly screamed hysterically. All of us froze and none dared utter a word. Panic ensued as we looked about for him frantically.

"There he is!" someone shouted, pointing to the little boy as he made his way toward one group of wild animals near the water.

Story analysis – showing and telling

The story has a beginning (the introduction to my accommodation in the evening), a middle (the breakfast the following morning and the trip on the way to the safari), and an ending (the scene by the watering hole and the dramatic climax). The main characters are the narrator and little boy.

We go straight to the scene of the action from the start, skipping any details about planning or booking the holiday, as this is not important to the flow of the story. It is a good idea to provide as much palpable detail as possible, zooming in and describing things that would capture the reader's attention. I described the bungalow and its surroundings in some detail.

Reveal, directly or indirectly, the characters' thoughts, feelings and opinions about people, places and things; this will help the readers/listeners form a rapport with them.

The main character of this story, besides the narrator, is the little boy. I introduce him in the second scene at the breakfast table (although I briefly mention his tantrums earlier), but then I leave the thread open. This method creates suspense: we want to know more about the boy.

The journey, by open top vehicle, to the safari spot is an action scene. Action scenes need not be dramatic, however, they do need to move the story forward. In it I ratcheted up the misbehaviour of the boy, foreshadowing what was to occur in the final scene.

In the final scene, there is surprise, as the focus is initially on the entrance of the lion, then the focus moves abruptly and alarmingly to the disappearance of the little boy.

The story ends on an open loop, leaving what happens to him unresolved.

(e) Show using dialogue

The mannerisms with which people speak can give us lots of information about their character: their moods, temperament, emotional state, feelings, thoughts, background, *etc.*

In the bar scene above, we can "show" how much John fancies the girl and how he flirts with her by using dialogue; for example:

> "Howdy, my name is John. Are you are on your own here? You're a bit of an early bird," he teased her. "What's your name?"

To take an entirely different example, you could "show" a woman is old by having her speak dialogue with a slow, croaky voice. Or, you could show that a person comes from a foreign country by their broken English and their accent; for example:

> "I come here when I had eighteen years. Miami it please me. Is good place for me."

In the field

There are certain times when you do need to "show" rather than "tell", especially when:

(a) **Telling stories**

In this case, feel free to embellish you story with plenty of (skilful) descriptions and (significant) details.

(b) **Demonstrating high value (DHV)**

> "I just bought a smashing sports car!"

"I've got a 10 bedroom house in the country."

"I only date models."

If you "tell" people about your life style like this, you will come across as braggart.

If you invest too much effort in "showing" them, however, that too can come across as bragging. Instead, show them with details, but embed them into a bigger story.

For example, if you want to "show" that your ex-girlfriend Julie was beautiful, then say something like:

"Whenever Julie entered the room, men's heads would turn as they checked her out."

"She was constantly getting hit on at parties, and guys would ask her out in front of me."

(c) **Proposing future dating adventures**
When you ask a girl out on a date, you should describe the venue and the activity to her. This is a good opportunity to "tell" her what you like about the place and to "show" her your past experiences. It could be a secluded area of a beach, a camping spot in the forest, your favourite meeting place, the café that serves the best coffee, *etc.*

Describe the things that make this place unique or special. It is also helpful to find out some of the things the girl might like to do there.

Exercises

Using colourful description and significant detail, "show" the listener or reader the following scenarios:

1. An old woman pacing about in her room.

2. A mafia boss you just did a deal with.

3. A fight scene in a bar.

4. A little girl playing with a doll and a doll house.

5. Your experience of a hobby or interest.

Include dialogue

Dialogue gives us an indication of what our characters are like and how their mood was at the time of the story being told. There are two types of dialogues – internal and external.

Internal dialogue is the conversation the character is having with himself – his inner game. External dialogue is the conversation he is having with the people around him – his outer game.

Dialogue should be used sparingly and everyday "chit-chat" should be avoided; for example, when we meet people in real life, we often resort to small talk and discuss trivial topics like the weather or what we had for dinner, *etc*. In a story, such topics would merely be a distraction.

There are three main reasons for using dialogue in a story:

161

(a) **To describe characters**

e.g. state of mind, accent, temperament, feelings, background.

> "If I ever see that man again, I am going to strangle him," Tim said.

(b) **To provide information**

> "To find the treasure, you must go through the forest and do not talk to anyone," the wizard told the boy as he pointed to the map.

(c) **To move the plot forward**

> "I am going to leave home and become a priest," the son suddenly exclaimed to his mother.

Make sure that each character has a distinct way of dialoguing, as this will form part of his identity. No two characters in your story should dialogue in quite the same manner; for example, a Mafia boss will speak in a different way from a homeless beggar.

14. Figures of speech

"Shall I compare thee to a summer's day?"
Shakespeare, Sonnet 18

We use comparisons in speech every day, even though we may not be aware of it. Using comparison effectively will greatly enhance you story telling skills and ability.

There are four main types of figures of speech: simile, metaphor, personification and hyperbole.

Simile

When describing something we may explicitly compare it to something else using comparison words:

"It was like ..."

For example, if a friend asked you how your date was, you might reply:

"The restaurant we went to was as posh as the Ritz."

"The girl acted like a little puppy."

"Her hair was like Goldilocks."

Description highlights certain aspects of our experiences in a colourful and interesting way. We use similes, however, in order to explicitly associate or compare significant details, with a different thing in a way that is eye-catching, using express words of comparison: "as" and "like".

Consider the following examples of "as" and "like" simile:

"As" statements	"Like" statements
He is as big as an elephant.	Your neck is like a tree trunk
The pan is as black as coal.	You have legs like twigs.
He is as brave as a lion.	Your hair is like soft silk.
The light is as bright as the sun.	Happy like a bird in flight.
She is as busy as a bee.	He is tall like a giant.
The water is as clear as crystal.	She is fast like a rocket.
The yoghurt is as cold as ice.	He is graceful like a swan.
It is as dead as the dodo.	She is sneaky like a fox.
She is as fat as a hippo.	He is quiet like a mouse.
He is as hard as nails.	He is fast like a bullet.

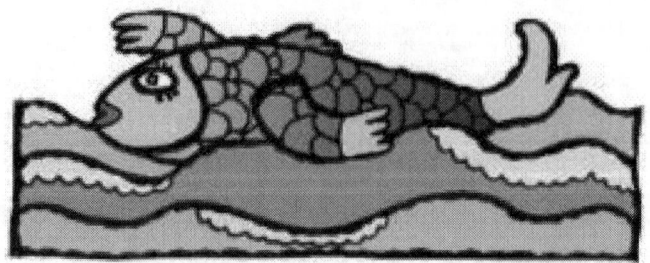

He swims as fast as a fish   He drinks like a fish

Avoid using *cliché* words with women, like rose, candle, star, *etc*.

164

How should you use similes in the field?

Again, suppose you just met a girl who seems positive about life; you might say to her:

"You radiate warmth and it lights up the room and encourages everyone around you. Your aura I'm sure is multi-coloured and attracts like-minded people toward you."

Suppose, you already know a girl who likes to travel and has decided to take a year off in order to do it. You might say to her,

"You are like a free-flying swallow ... (pause and wait for her response) ... that flies into the air of new adventures, flitting from place to place. You are about to spread your wings and leave your nest, saying goodbye to your family and friends and your younger siblings who are like the little chicks. Every experience and person you meet will be like a course of instruction that you can cherish forever."

You might gesture by:

- closing your upturned fist tight then suddenly opening it suggesting freedom and release, and

- waving your hands up and down suggesting the flapping of wings.

You have to make your delivery – playful, teasing and fun. Do not be serious!

Exercise

Use similes to describe these types whom you might meet in the field, writing one paragraph each:

(a) A girl who likes to do a lot of shopping.

(b) A man who is academically inclined and likes to spend time reading.

Also, describe any associated gestures you might while telling the story to an audience.

Metaphors

> *"All the world's a stage and men and women merely players"* **Shakespeare**

Metaphor is a type of comparison, like simile, but less explicit: it avoids comparison words: "as" "like" *etc.* Metaphorical comparisons tend to be stronger because it tends to compare wholes rather than just single features. You would use metaphor to try and create the impression of a stronger resemblance between otherwise dissimilar things. With metaphor we conflate two things, but with simile the two items remain distinct; for example, in the dating event in the simile section, we might have used metaphors to say something like:

"She was a princess!"

"Her skin was peachy."

"It was heavenly."

"She was Goldilocks."

To take the master example in the quotation from Shakespeare, the metaphor has these parts:

- The world is a stage (as with a set script).

- Men and women are actors (as if playing out their roles).

Below are examples of metaphors:

- The young girl is an angel.

- Tom is an Einstein.

- He was a lion in the fight.

- That offer was music to my ears.

- His plans were rock-solid and so were his aims.

- He was rubbing his paws all over me.

- She was a typhoon on the ice skating ring.

- James is a jolly giant.

Exercises

Use metaphor to describe these types, whom you might meet in the field:

(a)   A teenage girl who parties a lot (like a social butterfly).

(b)   A guy who is dress to get attention women (like a peacock).

Personification

Personification is an indirect comparison that confers on an inanimate object the characteristics, traits, qualities, attributes, actions and feeling of an animate being. We use personification to take objects and "bring them to life" to make them more interesting and to make them stand out.

There are several things you can personify:

(a)   **Objects**

"The sun smiled at the landscape."

"The sun was playing hide-and-seek from behind the clouds."

"The waves wrapped me in their strong arm."

(b) **Animals**

"The bees were bringing in the harvest from the late summer gardens."

"Poised to strike, the snake had me in its viewfinder."

(c) **Concepts and ideas**

"Time marches on."

"News travels quickly."

"Mother Nature is your best friend."

"The angry lightning danced across the sky."

You can give one object several human characteristics at a time; take a tree for example:

"The trees were thirsty for water."

"The trees fought with the strong winds."

"The tree was all dressed in green for the summer."

"The trees nodded in approval."

Below are examples of personifications:

"The rain kissed my cheeks as it fell."

"The printer spat out more copies than I needed."

"The flood waters swallowed up the trees."

"Fear gripped me as I heard footsteps."

"Snow had wrapped Stockholm in a white blanket."

"The tree beckoned the campers to its shade."

"Opportunity knocked."

The reader may have noticed that personification is a special case of a metaphor. It is also true that personification very often implies that the object personified is given a "role" to play throughout a story; but this more involved form of personification will not be used in this book.

Hyperbole

Hyperbole is used for purposes of exaggeration to extremes when comparing two things. It is often confused with simile and metaphor which it resembles and indeed would be except that it is not based on likeness. Some hyperboles are used so often that they have become *clichés*.

Below are some examples of hyperboles:

"I nearly died laughing."

"I walked a million miles."

"I called you a thousand times."

"The bags weighed a tonne."

"I'm so hungry I could eat a horse."

"He has got loads of money."

"I'm so tired I could sleep all week."

"It is raining cats and dogs."

James is growing so fast, soon he'll be taller than the trees.

James is growing so fast, soon he'll be reaching the clouds.

Real life example

Recently I was passing by my local Saturday street market and a new stall caught my attention. It was a French patisserie with neatly laid rows of delicious freshly baked cakes. I noticed that there were few people crowded around this store, merrily eyeing the goods on offer.

I opened a person next to me by saying:

"This looks a bit like bees around honey ..."

It immediately got the other person's attention and he started talking to me.

Try saying something different, instead of opening with a standard comment like:

"It looks good." or "Nice weather today."

15. Cold-readings, class 1 and class 2

People are typically unsure of themselves when they first start doing cold-readings. They worry about the reaction they might get from others.

For this reason, I would suggest starting with a template that has proven itself time and time again. There are two classes (sections) in this chapter, about Forer and Sundberg statements.

N.B. these readings are particularly effective when used on young students; *i.e.* teens and young folk in their early 20s.

Class 1: Using Forer statements

About Forer

In 1948 the psychologist B. Forer gave a sample of college students a battery of personality tests. He told them he would review their results and, based on that, he would produce an individual personality profile for each student the following week.

The students were eager to receive their profiles and were told they had to gauge how accurately the profiles reflected their personalities. Overall, the students rated the profiles as 84% accurate.

However, what Forer did not tell the students was that he had returned to all of them an identical profile, which consisted of the same 13 statements. He had simply looked up these statements in newspaper horoscopes, completely disregarding the actual test results in favour of these 13 "Forer statements".

These same tests has been tried out on students in the past 60 years since Forer's pioneering experiment, and it still yields positive feedback in the +80 % range!

The main reasons why Forer statements work so well are:

1. They are general comments that could apply to anyone and everyone.
    For example, telling someone, "You have a tendency to over-think".

2. People tend to personalise general statements as being about themselves.
    So, the person told a Forer statement will assume it is specifically related to herself.

3. The statements are either neutral or complimentary. This reduces the chances of its being rejected.

    Such generalised statements are seen every day in horoscopes.

Sagittarius (Nov ...... imagination because they leave out the uneventful moments. In real life, hours, weeks or years might pass between major developments. Be happy you're here to experience the whole thing.

CAPRICORN (Dec 22 - Jan 19):You have many good friends who don't get along with each other. Leave the peacemaking for someone else and be happy in your role as a go-between. Others will join you once they share your taste for variety.

Aquarius (Jan 20 - Feb 18):Personalities don't change much over the course of a lifetime. Today's fashion won't look the same next week. Be patient with someone who says they've seen it all before. Some trends are circular in nature.

Here are the 13 statements Forer used:

"You have a great need for other people to like and admire you. You have a tendency to be critical of yourself. You have a great deal of unused capacity which you have not turned to your advantage. While you have some personality weaknesses, you are generally able to compensate for them. Your sexual adjustment has presented some problems for you. Disciplined and self-controlled outside, you tend to be worrisome and insecure inside. At times you have serious doubts as to whether you have made the right decision or done the right thing. You prefer a certain amount of change and variety and become dissatisfied when hemmed in by restrictions and limitations. You pride yourself as an independent thinker and do not accept others' statements without satisfactory proof. You have found it unwise to be too frank in revealing yourself to others. At times you are

174

extroverted, affable, sociable, while at other times you are introverted, wary, reserved. Some of your aspirations tend to be pretty unrealistic. Security is one of your major goals in life."

Transition to the cold-reading

If I was chatting with a person I had never met before, I might use a cold-reading on her later on in our interaction. Initially, I would like to study and get to know her as much as possible. I would then use all this information (dress sense, tone of voice, bodily attitude, the question she asks) for making small and obvious cold-readings about her.

During our conversation, I might drop hints that I am into "esoterica" – yoga, meditation, energy fields, mind/body/spirit, world religions, healing, nutrition, *etc.*

This enables me to gauge, how receptive she might be to a cold-reading.

If the receptivity is indicated, at some point I would take her right hand and say –

"Let me see ...

... I like it to be quiet when I am reading a person's energy."

You have to be confident with your delivery. Also keep good eye contact with her and watch her responses carefully.

Yes ladder

Salesmen often use the "Yes ladder". He starts off posing queries or assertions everyone would agree to, which is designed to get the customer to say "yes" as many times as possible. According to the "commitment and consistency" principle, the person who says "yes" to small things is likelier to continue saying "yes" to larger requests. Thus, the salesman has better chances to close the deal.

We can use these same principles with the opposite sex. The more times we can get him/her to say "yes" in the beginning, the likelier he/she will continue to say "yes". In cold-reading lingo a client saying "yes" is what is called a "hit". Just remember that you must give reasons for making these comments (called "grounding") by adding words like "because" and "as".

For example, I once met an *au-pair* from Germany who was in London for six months. She was taking time off from her studies as a primary school teacher.

I was able to make these initial cold-readings which she agreed with:

> "You take your education and studies seriously ... because you are studying at university."

> "You are independent and prepared to take risks if required ... as you have been living abroad for some time."

> "You are a patient person ... because you work with young children."

> "You are caring and nurturing ... as you like working with people."

Moulding

Cold-readings can even be used to mould a person into the character type we are seeking.

I next made the following statements to the German *au-pair*:

> "You are open to meeting new people and to new experiences."

> "You are an open-minded person."

> "You have a sense of adventure in you that needs to be brought out"

After you have made a few mini-cold-readings, you can go on to the medium-length cold-readings; *i.e.* the Forer statements.

A detailed look

When we look at these statements in detail, we notice that:

1. The statements are general and vague, as mentioned above.

2. They reflect human nature and behaviour, in general.

3. The language cannot be quantified; for example, "a great need", "a tendency", "at times", "a certain amount", *etc.*

4. They are positive or at worst neutral – people are more likely to rate positive statements as accurate as applied to themselves.

5. In sum, you are telling people what they want to hear.

Let's see what we might say about each of these 13 statements:

1. *"You have a great need for other people to like and admire you."*

Everyone has a need for acceptance and love from others. People like attention and validation from others and it is important to them.

2. *"You have a tendency to be critical of yourself."*

Most people do tend to be hard on themselves, more than on others. Most of us have a lot of negative self-talk going through our heads and beat ourselves up from time to time.

3. *"You have a great deal of unused capacity which you have not turned to your advantage."*

This is an interesting statement. It allows the person to interpret it any which way they want; that is, they can invest it with whatever meaning is applicable to their own individual lives.

4. *"While you have some personality weaknesses, you are generally able to compensate for them."*

This is a type of cold-reading called the "rainbow ruse", which deploys both a given character trait (in this case, weaknesses) and its opposite (in this case, strengths), so something is bound to apply.

5. *"Your sexual adjustment has presented some problems for you."*

This is an unusual statement, but bear in mind that it was written 60 years ago. It has to been brought up to date.

For starters, I would avoid using the word "sex" or using any sexual references with people you have just met. You might start by bringing up romantic themes; for example, if she is single, you might suggest that she will soon find her Prince Charming.

6. *"Disciplined and self-controlled outside, you tend to be worrisome and insecure inside."*

This is another rainbow ruse. It is also a statement that applies generally to a lot of women, as they tend to worry and feel insecure.

7. *"At times you have serious doubts as to whether you have made the right decision or done the right thing."*

This is a clever statement that relies on universal experiences like hindsight (in the first half) and decision making (in the second half).

8. *"You prefer a certain amount of change and variety and become dissatisfied when hemmed in by restrictions and limitations."*

Who doesn't like variety in their lives? However, it is vague and does not specify the type of change or variety. At this point you might suggest that she is in need of a holiday or travel adventure.

Again, most people do like their freedom and do not like being told what to do or not do. This is especially relevant in the context of relationships between young people and parents or teachers.

9. *"You pride yourself as an independent thinker and do not accept others' statements without satisfactory proof."*

This is compliment and flattery, which of course people warm to.

10. *"You have found it unwise to be too frank in revealing yourself to others."*

This statement will be recognised by all as applicable to oneself: who has not been embarrassed by confidences betrayed? "Once burnt, twice shy" the saying goes, and people will always have secrets that they would be unwise to reveal to just anyone.

11. *"At times you are extroverted, affable, sociable while at other times you are introverted, wary, reserved."*

This is another classic rainbow ruse.

12. *"Some of your aspirations tend to be pretty unrealistic."*

Everyone has unrealistic ambitions and aspirations that cannot be satisfied.

This is also a "negative" statement that is thrown in to help make the cold-reading sound more authentic, believable and plausible.

13. *"Security is one of your major goals in life."*

People in general are inherently insecure, and are always looking for security and stability.

Class 2: Using Sundberg statements

While you are still a beginner at doing cold-readings, I suggest that you use Forer statement. Here on the other hand is an alternative model that has been tried, tested and proved on college students successful over decades.

About Sundberg

In 1955, about eight years after the Forer experiments, N. D. Sundberg gave a sample of students the Minnesota Multiphasic Personality Inventory (MMPI), a standardized test used by psychologists to inventory personality. From the test results personality profiles for each of the students were written up by psychologists.

Then each student was presented with their real personality profile and a fake one. When asked to pick the more accurate profile, 60% of the students picked the fake one.

There are two important points to note about how people react to cold-readings:

1. People are less flattered and less willing to believe an accurate profile of their personality, with all of its real flaws; and

2. Most people prefer a pleasurable deception to the truth, especially if applied to themselves.

Sundberg statements

Here are the eight statements that Sundberg used:

"You appear to be a cheerful, well-balanced person. You may have some alternation of happy and unhappy moods, but they are not extreme now. You have few or no problems with your health. You are sociable and mix well with others. You are adaptable to social situations. You tend to be adventurous. Your interests are wide. You are fairly self-confident and usually think clearly."

A detailed look

When we look at these statements in detail, we notice once again that:

1. The statements are general and vague, as mentioned above.

2. They reflect human nature and behaviour, in general.

3. The language cannot be quantified; for example "a great need", "a tendency", "at times", "a certain amount" *etc.*

4. The statements are mainly positive or neutral – and people are more likely to rate positive statements as accurately applicable to themselves.

5. Once again, you tell them what they want to hear.

Let's see what we might say about each of these eight statements:

1. *"You appear to be a cheerful, well-balanced person"*

This is nothing but a positive statement. You could possibly mould the person into someone who is fun to be with. The words "well-balanced" refer to someone who is not extreme, one way or the other as most people are not.

2. *"You may have some alternation of happy and unhappy moods, but they are not extreme now"*

This is a "rainbow ruse" cold-reading. It is of course universally true that people's emotions alternate between happy and sad, through all gradations in between. The last half of the statement reinforces positive judgement that he/she is "balanced".

3. *"You have few or no problems with your health"*

Most young people are in good health, so this is sure to be accurate most of the time. You can go a bit farther and mention that:

- things can change in the future, as far as health is concerned, and

- there is inner health (*e.g.* peace, calm, relaxation, spirituality) and outer health.

The word "few" even covers the possibility that he/she could have some health problems.

4. *"You are sociable and mix well with others"*

Young people need social approval and prefer to consider themselves at least potentially popular. The second half of the statement flatteringly suggests that he/she gets on well with others and is well liked in turn.

5. *"You are adaptable to social situations"*

This follows from the statement above and is equally vague and generic; but it implies more about the person's relationships. It could mean any of the following:

- he/she is a team player,

- he/she is cooperative and communicative,

- he/she is a good "agony aunt", or

- he/she can connect with people and empathises well.

6. *"You tend to be adventurous"*

This is another flattering vague generality that could mean several things that might apply to nearly everyone, for example:

- he/she is independent,

- he/she likes to travel, or

- he/she is ambitious.

It is best to "ground" this statement, by giving reasons why you think this; for example:

- he/she has left home and is now living on a university campus, or

- he/she has moved to another country for a job

You can also use this to mould a shy girl into something a bit more like you may want her to be.

7. *"Your interests are wide"*

This is yet another flattering generality. The word "interests" suggest great many things of very widespread applicability; for example:

- he/she has any of a practically infinite number of hobbies and spare-time interests,

- he/she likes variety in her life,

- he/she is creative,

- he/she is imaginative, or

- he/she likes doing different things.

8. *"You are fairly self-confident and usually think clearly"*

This too is a positive, encouraging statement of the type that people prefer to hear.

Most young people tend to lack confidence, and are buoyed by such an assessment.

You are also praising their mental abilities – sure to be a generally accurate observation as youth is the age at which people are most likely to be enrolled in academic endeavours.

Closing

You should leave him/her wanting to know more. So, be sure to leave lots of open loops in your cold-readings.

Hopefully, he/she will want to see you again, and then you can reveal more to him/her.

16. Three common questions: Name? Do? From?

Three of the most habitual questions in a conversation are:

"What is your name?"

"Where are you from?"

"What do you do for a living?"

As these three questions are standard, you need to have your answers prepared in case you are asked. You also need to know how to respond to replies to your questionings. Consider the two possible scenarios:

1. *She asks you*

"Where are you from?"

This gives you an opportunity to tell her about all the special and unique aspects of the place you are from and what you like/dislike about it.

You can also get out your camera and show her pictures of where you live, then get her to guess the name of the place.

"What do you do for a living?"

It is best to avoid giving your job title (engineer, consultant, accountant, *etc.*) as she may not know what it means and might even stereotype you. Instead describe the positives of your role in words that are easy to understand (*e.g.* use analogies) and make you sound important. She is giving you a good chance to demonstrate high value (DHV); for example:

You reply: "I get called in by large companies to fix their sticky tech problems ... This involves travelling around European cities once a month and meeting lots of new and interesting people, as well as opportunities to make public presentations which I thoroughly enjoy."

Throw into the role things that you would like to do or can see yourself doing in the foreseeable future.

2. *You ask her*

"Where are you from?"

She replies:

"Madrid".

There are several ways in which you can reply to this; for example:

"I've never been to Madrid, but I'd like to go there someday soon. What three things would you recommend about the place?"

Or:

"Madrid! That's where all the beautiful women come from!"

Or:

"You know what they say about the girls from Madrid!"

Or:

"Is it true what they say about women from Madrid?"
(Better have a comeback ready in case she replies, "No,
what do they say?")

You: "What do you do for a living?"

Girl: "I'm a nurse."

There are several avenues you could pursue in response; for
example, you could elicit her values:

"You must be a caring and patient person in order to be a
nurse."

Or:

"What influenced you most in favour of becoming a nurse?"
(instead of asking how she got into it)

Or:

"If you could have any job you wanted, what would it be?"
(instead of asking if she likes her job)

What's in a name?

The first point to note is that people have a tendency to forget names when they are introduced. One way to remember another person names is to use it several time in a conversation. Also, people love to hear their own names.

The other point is that if you want your name to be remembered, you should attach a short additional line to it. For myself, I would say, "My name is Osmond. It's funny how people always remember my name. It must be unique."

17. Cosmo conversation: Girls with guns

One way to gain information to use in conversation is by reading women's and men's magazines like Cosmopolitan, Elle, Marie Claire, GQ, *etc.* The advantages of reading such magazines are:

(a) The articles are current.
     Usually, only the most up-to-date information is published.

(b) The articles are interesting.
     Lots of people are addicted to this stuff.

(c) They have a wide readership, so that people you meet are likely to have heard of or read about the same topics.

You need to look at these magazines fairly regularly, and glean a few articles of interest from each one. Thus, looking through a recent edition of one of them, an article was found with the title:

"Girls with guns"

The sub-title reads:

> "Across America, firearms are fast becoming a must-have accessory. But is this fear of serious crime justified or a sign of a society in the grip of intense paranoia?"

You always need to select the emotive articles and read through them carefully.

Topic and sub-topics

Carefully make note of the topics and sub-topics. Jot down key points of interest and do not let yourself get bogged down in the detail. Stay away from negative or grizzly topics.

The topic of this article is girls carrying guns in the USA.

The sub-topics are several:

- rising crime in today's society,

- self-defence and personal security,

- "paranoia",

- things getting out of control,

- gun rights, and

- girl power.

Background research

The more background research you do, the better you will be prepared to hold attention-getting and socially effective conversations about topics of interest to many of the people you will meet. And, you will become more successful at being assertive with anyone and at putting your views across.

However, *N.B.*:

1. It is pointless having a discussion or debate on a topic you know little or nothing about.

2. The information you glean are "facts and figures", but you have to deliver it in an interesting and absorbing way, *i.e.* by storytelling and "showing".

The research done on the above topic, also yielded other information of general interest:

*   Police in the UK do not carry guns. Carrying handguns in the UK is illegal.

*   The Second Amendment to the US Constitution allows citizens to carry guns.

*   The firearms lobby is strong in the USA.

*   There are an estimated 200 million privately owned guns in the USA.

*   Open Carry (OC) is a new and controversial movement, is for carrying guns, so that it is visible; its members tend to be women who frequent local establishments like Starbucks.

*   Some restaurants and cafes in the USA have now banned the carrying of guns on their premises.

Transition

You must learn how to transition smoothly from one topic of conversation another.

N.B.: A transition is a "smooth hook" that leads gently into the new topic or thread.

You can try these hooks, for example:

"My friend in America wrote to me about ..."

"I read about this in the newspapers the other day ..."

"Did you watch that programme on telly about ...?"

"When I was in LA/NYC last year ..."

Questions to ask

When conversing about the latest topics, always try to ask questions that will interest, intrigue and challenge your interlocutors; for example:

1. "Which side of the debate do you stand on – for the right to carry guns openly or against?"

2. "Do you think carrying guns is empowering for women?"

3. "Is this the best way for women to defend themselves?"

4. "If you were carrying a gun concealed in your handbag would you be able to get it out in time in case you needed it?"

5. "Do you think guns and shooting in movies, the media and computer games, influences violence in people?"

6. "Would you carry a gun on your first date?"

Mix serious questions with humorous ones.

You should tailor such questions to elicit a definite response, and to hint that you have thought through the topic carefully.

The general rule is that you should ask specific, direct questions. This will result in a good and socially useful response. Avoid asking general and cliché type questions.

Think of it as being like when a patient visits a doctor: even though the patient will describe his/her ailment and some of its symptoms, the doctor will ask specific questions nonetheless to pinpoint it.

Your opinions count

You do not have to agree with everything the other person says. Avoid being a "yes" man. State your opinions and give reasons to back up your case.

18. My blog: writing about life experiences

Whenever you visit interesting places or do unusual things, always if possible take notes and photos of the event. This will provide lots of grist for conversation. Use real life experiences in your conversation whenever possible, as these will be what you will speak with the most passion about.

Your conversation should always reflect your character and experiences, but is not intended that you should be like a "tour guide". As an example, the following describes three venues that I have visited and like to talk about from time to time.

1. Covent Garden, Central London

Before you introduce a new topic of conversation, make sure you can make it an interesting one.

Before you can make a topic interesting, you will have to have done fun things. As an example, I am going to write about a precinct area that has been at the heart of London for over 500 years and attracts millions of tourists and visitors every year.

I like meeting in this area for a coffee, so I have made sure that I am "well-armed" to describe it to people in an interesting way, both before and during our meeting.

1. *Topic and sub-topics*

You need to carefully make a list of your topics and its sub-topics. Make a note of the key points of interest and do not get bogged down in the detail. Stay away from any negatives, and avoid reciting too many facts and figures.

The topic is Covent Garden.

The possible sub-topics might include, for example:

- history of the area,

- tourist attraction,

- type of shops/stores,

- atmosphere, and

- places to eat and relax.

2. *Background research*

The more background knowledge you have, the better prepared you will be to converse effectively about the topic. Also, you will get better at being assertive and with putting your views across.

The research on this topic included:

The history of Covent Garden
The name Covent Garden derives from the garden of a convent that belonged to Westminster Abbey and its monks in the middle ages. It was officially titled "the garden of the Abbey and Convent of Westminster".

After Henry VIII seized all of the Catholic Church's estates and monasteries in 1539, when he first set up the Church of England, the lands of the convent garden together with Long Acre became property of the crown. This land the king granted to John Russell, 1st Earl of Bedford (see picture below).

The land eventually descended to Francis Russell, the 4th Earl of Bedford. He commissioned Inigo Jones (see picture below), the greatest architect of the time, to develop it architecturally and to build houses on the site that would be "fit for the habitations of gentlemen".

The piazza was laid out in 1630 and was inspired by the spacious squares of Italian and French city centres. This piazza was the first of its kind in England, and was a big hit with visitors. It featured a cobbled square and surrounding streets that formed a straight grid pattern, unlike the haphazardly twisting streets elsewhere in London.

West side of Covent Garden – St Paul's Church

The Tuscan portico of St. Paul's Church forms the principal focus on the west side of the Piazza. This too was designed by Inigo Jones.

The church itself is back to front, so to speak. The door beneath the portico was supposed to be the entrance according to the architectural canons, but that would have meant facing the congregation in the western or wrong direction. Thus, the back door became the main entrance.

The very first victim of the Great Plague of 1665 – one Margaret Ponteous, a doctor's daughter – was buried in the churchyard at St Paul's on 12th April 1665, the cause of death being given briefly in the church register as "PLA". Unbeknownst to those in attendance, her death portended the start of the worst plague in London's history.

South side – the fruit and vegetable market

This began in a very small way in 1649 but soon it expanded in response to the Great Fire of London of 1666 which destroyed the markets of the (old Roman) City of London directly to the east.

The stalls of market traders hawking fruits and vegetables grew to be a characteristic feature of the square, and the 4th Earl of Bedford, shrewdly recognising the business potential of a market sited in between the City of London and Westminster, obtained the right to hold it by Letters Patent from King Charles II in 1670.

The original market, consisting of wooden stalls and sheds, became disorganised and disorderly, and the 6th Earl of Bedford requested an Act of Parliament in 1813 to regulate it; then commissioned Charles Fowler in 1830 to design the neo-classical market building that is the heart of Covent Garden today.

This market has been relocate to Nine Elms in Vauxhall (see below) and replaced with shops, cafes and an arts and crafts market called the "Apple market".

North-east side – Royal Opera House
The Covent Garden Theatre, now the Royal Opera House, opened in 1733, built by John Rich with the aid of public subscriptions.

Transition

If you need to make a smooth transition from another topic of conversation to this one, you could use a hook like this:

"Covent Garden is my favourite place to meet in London!"

"Covent Garden has an amazing history."

Questions to ask

Her answer to the following questions will depend on her interest in the area and whether she has seen the sights. Some good questions to ask:

"Have you been to Covent Garden?"

"What do you like to shop for in Covent Garden?"

"What is your favourite part of the Covent Garden area?"

Your opinions count

You do not have to agree with everything the girl/guy says. Avoid being her yes-man. You can state your opinions and give reasons to back up your case.

Further topics for discussion

You can take the topic further and talk about related topics like:

(a) **Seven Dials**
Seven Dials was originally laid out by Thomas Neale, M.P, in the early 1690s, upon his devising the characteristic

"seven dials" street layout in order to maximise the number of houses that could be built on the site and his profit.

(b) **New Covent Garden Market**

Covent Garden continued to host sellers of fruit and flowers, vegetables and herbs, for more than three hundred years. By the end of the 1960s traffic congestion had become a problem. An Act of Parliament in 1966 mandated relocation of Covent Garden Market to new premises at Nine Elms, Vauxhall, eight years later. This is now the largest fruit, vegetable and flower market in the UK.

(c) **Punch and Judy show**

These are the world-renowned two-hand puppets created by Samuel Pepys in 1662. There is also a large pub of the same name at Covent Garden.

(d) **London Transport Museum**

Originally the Flower Market, the first part of the market was put up in 1872 by William Rogers. The museum replaced the flower market in 1980. The flower market has been relocated to the New Covent Garden market in Nine Elms, Vauxhall.

(e) **Neal's Yard**

Neal's Yard, now home to a cluster of vegetarian cafes, new age shops and homeopathic remedy stores, has attracted alternative medicine dealers, occultists and astrologers since the 17th Century.

(f) *"My Fair Lady"*

Covent Garden was used as the backdrop for the musical play and film *"My Fair Lady"*.

The Royal Opera House (though it wasn't known as such at the time) has been immortalized in the beloved musical *My Fair Lady* based on *Pygmalion, the play* by George Bernard Shaw. In the opening scene of the 1964 movie, the credits roll against a background of opera-goers leaving the theatre and a couple of scenes later Dr. Henry Higgins, professor of phonetics, meets a poor Covent Garden flower-girl, Eliza Doolittle, under one of the arcades along the Covent Garden piazza.

The stage version of *My Fair Lady* premiered in New York in 1956 and at the Theatre Royal, Drury Lane in London in 1958. The reviews hailed the show as a triumph and it went on to break all box office records. The film was nominated for 12 Oscars, won eight and remains a classic to this day.

Performers on the piazza in front of the church. The Punch and Judy pub is in the middle of the photo. Jubilee market and Apple market is to the right and Covent Garden subway is to the left.

2. Olympic park adventure

Another example is the newly opened Olympic Park, which I was invited by friends to visit before the sporting events started. We spent about three hours touring and filming the park. The weather was overcast and drizzly.

Topic and sub-topics

Once again, take care to list the topics and the sub-topics. Note the key points of interest and avoid too much detail, and eschew negatives.

The topic is the Olympic Park.

The possible sub-topics might include, for example:

- building the Park,

- venues and locations,

- type of sport involved,

- legacy after the event,

- construction works,

- history of the grounds,

- countries taking part, and

- visitors and tourists in London.

Background research

As noted before, background knowledge will prepared you to converse about the topic in ways that interest others. It will also help you at being assertive and putting your views across.

Research on this event included:

- The Olympic Park is as big as Hyde Park or 350 football pitches.

- It took seven years of planning and construction to build, from July 2005 to July 2012.

- Much of the site was initially disused and derelict, while parts of it were already occupied by houses and old factories.

- Several other venues, in and around London hosted events, e.g. sailing was at Weymouth.

- London had hosted the Olympic Games twice before in 1908 and 1948.

- The Olympic Village inside Olympic park provided accommodation for athletes and officials during the Games.

- It was the first Olympic Park to feature nature and wildlife, and its grounds included flowers, birds, woodlands and rivers/ponds.

- The soil was heavily contaminated and had to be cleaned before the park could be built.

- An Energy Centre was constructed on the western side of the Olympic Park to provide a low-carbon heating and cooling system across the site not only for the Games but also for the new buildings and communities that will be developed after 2012.

- Security was a major issue, with many military and policemen on duty.

- The legacy of the Olympic Park will be quite substantial: it will become the site of the largest urban park created in Europe for more than 150 years; a new university will be founded on it; the Stadium is expected be taken over by West Ham United FC; the permanent sporting arena – such as the VeloPark and Aquatics centre – will be open to the public and used for competitions; Olympic Village will be converted into 3,600 apartments.

Transition

If you need ideas for making a smooth transition from another topic of conversation to this one, try one of these hooks:

"Did you watch the Olympics ...?"

"I read about the Olympic Park in the newspapers the other day ..."

"The other day on telly I saw something about the Olympic Park."

Questions to ask

The answers to the following questions will depend on the other person's interest in the event and whether he/she has seen the sights. Here are some good questions to ask:

"What did you like about the opening ceremony?"

"Which venue did you like the best? (and why?)"

"Which event did you like to watch the most? (really caught your eye?)"

"What do you think of the eco-friendly style of the 2012 Olympics?"

"Are you the sporty type?"

"Do you know what the hand signals mean in beach volleyball?"

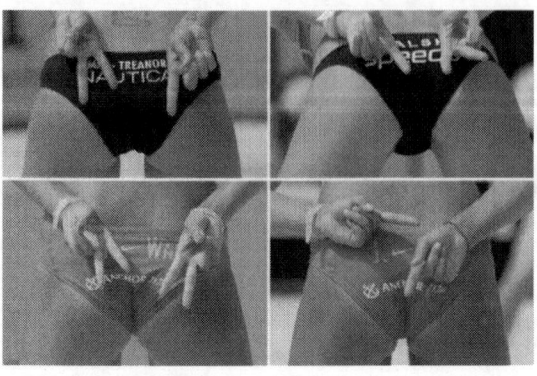

Your opinions count

As usual, you need not agree with everything the other person says. Avoid being a yes man. You can state your opinions assertively.

Further topics for discussion

You take this topic further and talk about other related topics, such as:

1948 Austerity Olympics

You can compare the London Olympics of 2012 with the one previous in 1948. This does bid fair to make for an interesting topic of conversation, as the times were different back then. 1948 was the second time the UK had hosted the Olympics. By the bye, the UK is the only country ever to have hosted the Games three time. 1948 was called the "Austerity Olympics", as the UK had just come out of the World War II and was nearly broke. Rationing was still in place and the government could not afford to build any new venues for the Games or accommodation for the athletes.

Other points of interest you can mention:

- British athletes could not afford equipment and proper training facilities.
- Food for the athletes was rationed.
- Athletes were housed in army barracks or education colleges.
- Germany and Japan were not allowed to participate because of their role in the war.
- The total cost of the Games was only £ 750,000.

- Some equipment had to be borrowed from other countries.
- The British flag for the Opening Ceremony had been forgotten and left behind, yet famed-distance runner Roger Bannister managed to get it there on time.

Events and players

You might talk about the sport you like best and who your favourite athletes are. Be prepared to talk about what you like about the:

- Individual athletes
  What inspires you about an athlete?
  Do you have any interesting background information about him/her?

- Particular sports
  Have you played this sport in the past?
  What do you like about it?
  Did you watch an event on telly that you like to talk about?

The Rio Games

You might also say something about the Olympic Games in Rio in 2016. It will be the first time that a South American (and Portuguese speaking) country has hosted the games.

The competition venues will be clustered in four zones – Barra (will host the main events and will house the Olympic village), Copacabana, Deodoro and Maracanã – and connected by a high-performance transport ring. The southern neighbourhood of Copacabana, with its famous 4km beach, will be the site for rowing, sailing and athletics, canoeing, kayaking and beach volleyball.

There are on-going problems with crime and security and this is bound to affect the visitors from overseas. The authorities are working closely with the poorer districts (*i.e.* favelas).

The official Rio 2016 Logo is made up of three figures embracing, with the overall shape reflecting the city's famous landmark, Sugarloaf Mountain. It depicts the three colours of the Brazilian flag, blue, green and yellow.

Memorable points about the London Olympic Park

Olympic Stadium

- Olympic Stadium has a capacity of 80,000.
- It is the lightest-weight Olympic stadium ever built.
- Fourteen lighting towers were needed because this was the first Olympic Games with HD TV freeze-frame coverage, and good lighting was essential to capture the action.
- Part of the supporting structure of the roof is formed of 2,500 tonnes of steel tubing that was actually recycled from old gas pipelines.

Velodrome

- The Velodrome is one of the most sustainable venues in the Olympic Park. The lightweight roof weighs only half that of any other covered velodrome, which contributed along with other cutting-edge features to make a highly-efficient building.
- The Velodrome's 'Cable net' roof is made of 17 kilometers of steel cables. That is more than 10 miles of steel cable, twice the height of Mount Everest.
- The designers and builders of the Velodrome were aiming to create the fastest indoor cycling track in the world.

Aquatics Centre

- The steel used to build the Aquatics centre comes from Newport in Wales.
- The wave shaped roof measures 12,000 square metres which is one and a half times the size of the Wembley football pitch.
- The amount of material that had to be excavated to build the Aquatics centre was the equivalent of 160,000 tonnes of soil.

Basketball Arena

- Referred to as "marshmallow" because of its shape.
- The arena is recyclable and will be demolished and recycled in 2013.
- Its construction was from lightweight steel frames and cladding.

International Broadcast/Main Press Centre

- The International Broadcast Centre will be a 24 hour media hub for the approximately 20,000 broadcasters, photographers and journalists who will bring the Games to an estimated four billion people worldwide.
- The Centre is the size of six full sized football pitches.
- The biggest fork lift truck in the country was used to help erect the steel frame.

Truly interesting topics of conversation never become "dated"; they do not come with a "time" stamp or expiry. Although the 2012 Olympics is now history, you can still bring it up in conversation any time you wish by using transitions like those exampled above.

N.B. Intrinsically interesting topics will always be of interest to most people.

3. Camden Market trail

I live nearby Camden Market and frequent the place. It is the fourth-most popular tourist attraction in London, drawing a crowd of approximately 100,000 people every weekend. This is a particularly good topic to bring up with people who have never visited it.

Topic and sub-topics

List the topics and its sub-topics, noting of the key points of interest. Avoid too much detail, negatives, and excessive facts and figures.

The topic is Camden Market.

The possible sub-topics might include, for example:

- history of the market,

- type of shops/stores,

- crowds and tourists,

- atmosphere, and

- places to eat and relax

Background research

Sufficient background knowledge prepares you to talk effectively about the topic, and incidentally teaches you to be more assertive and to put views across articulately.

The research done for this topic included:

The history of the market

The borough and town of Camden took its name from the 1st Earl of Camden, Charles Pratt (see picture below), who developed this neighbourhood of London in the early 1800s. The area had been a mere transit point to other locations north of London, like Hampstead, before this.

In the 1870s, Regent's Canal was built and around this the Lock Market was built. The canal attracted a lot of new business to the area resulting in its further development in the early 1900s. The goods-carrying barges were at first drawn by horses along the canal banks. However, this prosperity was short-lived, as roads and highways soon replaced waterways as the main medium of commercial transport.

In the 1970s three men, Bill Fulford, Peter Wheeler and Eric Roberts, came up with a plan to transform the area around Camden Lock into an arts and crafts market. The popularity of this small market grew and it now encompasses a number of distinct subsections, as detailed below.

When the canal was first being built, an experimental "hydro-pneumatic lock" was proposed to save water, which at the time was scarcely accessible for topping up the canal. The invention failed to work properly, and so conventional "double-locks" were installed, and are functioning today.

Camden Lock Market

This market is situated alongside Regent's Canal and is where the arts and crafts market was originally started in 1974. It has attracted huge numbers of visitors, partly due to the stalls being open on Sundays. Previous to the Sunday Trading Act 1994, shops were not permitted to be open for business on Sundays.

Stables Market

This part of the market used to be horse stables and a hospital for working horses, which used to treat horses injured pulling barges along the canal.

Chain stores and franchises are not permitted to trade in this area. It is the Mecca for shops selling furniture in the markets. Many of its stalls and shops are set into the large arches underneath railway viaducts.

Camden Lock village

This part of the market runs along the canal to the east of Chalk Farm Road. Visitors to the market usually sit along the banks and watch the boats go by.

Transition

To transition smoothly from another topic of conversation to this one, you can try this hook:

> "Couple of weeks ago, me and my friends were at Camden Market ..."

> "Funny you should mention shopping. That reminds me of Camden Market."

Questions to ask

The other person's answer to your questions will depend on their interest and whether he/she has seen the sights. Some good questions to ask are:

> "Have you ever been to Camden Market?"

"What do you like to shop for there?"

"What is your favourite section of it?"

"Do you prefer visiting the market during the weekdays or at the weekend?"

Focus-in on one of your favourites

There are many things to talk about touching Camden Market; however, in conversation it is best to focus-in on one sub-topic, which should be whatever it is about the topic that you like the most. Do not discuss too many things in detail, as this can confuse and overwhelm the listener.

Whenever I am in Camden, I frequent the InSpiral health food store and café. It is situated on a lovely spot beside the bridge and above the canal.

They have a selection of vegetarian hot food and salads. The dishes are healthy, organic and creative (for example, quinoa with mushroom pie).

They sell super-foods and raw products; the drinks and smoothies are delicious; for dessert they sell dairy-free ice cream and home-made raw food cakes.

Your opinions count

Make it a point not to agree with each and everything the other person says. You need not be anyone's yes-man; you are entitled to have your own opinions.

Further topics for discussion

To take this topic further, you can converse about related topics like:

(a) Farmers markets, in particular, about their importance and advantages/disadvantages compared to supermarkets
(b) Specialist markets *e.g.* antiques market, flower market, clothes market, food markets

The reasons you like to visit these types of markets and their history.

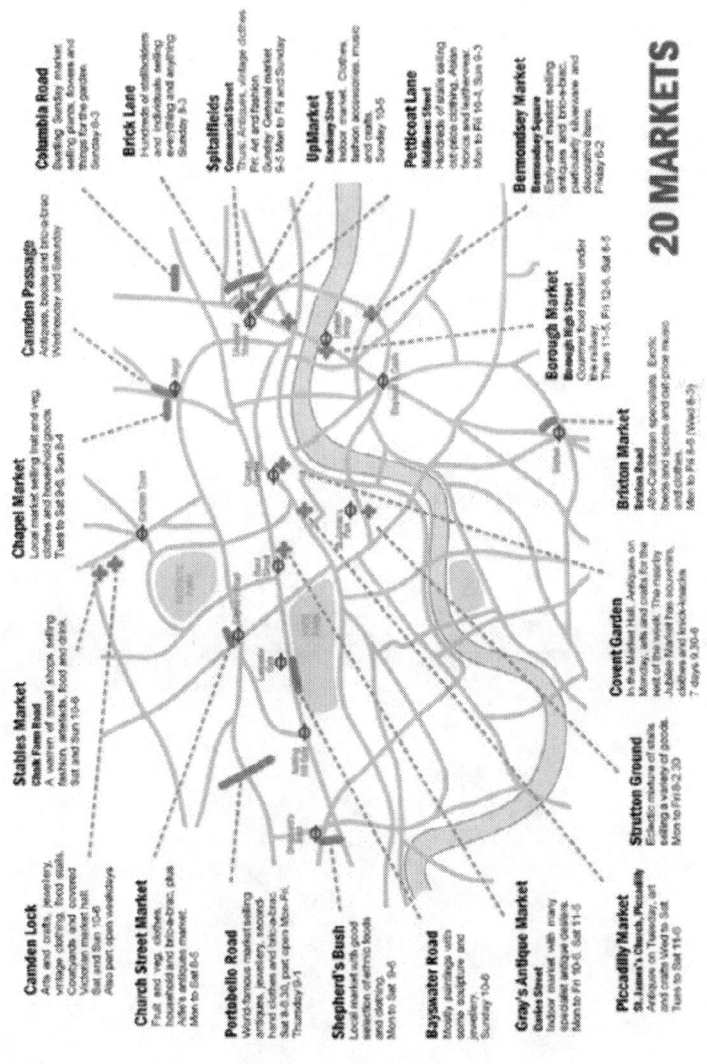

19. How to be assertive in conversations

Assertiveness is one of the new "buzz-words" we hear often these days. It is being used a lot in industry, in the work place, and in social situations. We would all benefit if we were more (truly) assertive in all our social interactions.

What is assertiveness?

Assertiveness is the habit of being free to express yourself authentically. It is about you being able to stand up for yourself and to say how you feel about anything. It is about staying true to your values, beliefs and standards in every situation in life.

Being assertive is a two-way street: at all times we need to respect the rights, needs, wants and views of the people we come in contact with.

Situation-dependency

Like confidence, assertiveness is situation dependent. We are better able to be assertive in some situations than in others; for example, with old friends it is easy to be assertive, but with the boss we may find it difficult.

Here are some situations where we would find it difficult to be assertive:

- talking with the opposite sex,

- meeting new people,

- job interviews,

- debating,

- public presentations (*e.g.* of a new business plan),

- public speaking in general,

- dealing with difficult people (*e.g.* neighbours), and

- dealing with those in authority (*e.g.* policemen, teachers).

Setting boundaries and standards

When people interact with you socially, they need and want to know where they stand with you.

You must set standards in all your conversations and relationships with people. You will gain respect if you keep up high standards, but lose it if you do not. At the same time, you need to have respect for other people's boundaries.

Make clear from the start that you will not tolerate such things as:

- lateness,

- rudeness,

- disrespectfulness,

- advantage-taking or overreaching, and

- dishonesty.

Be sure to call other people out if they do anything you are not happy with. You must make clear what action you will take if they continue misbehaving; *e.g.* " three times and you're out."

Avoid extremes

If you take assertiveness training, you will be told to avoid the extremes of passivity and aggression. Either of these extreme states, shows a lack of social and emotional intelligence.

Passive > > > > > > Assertive < < < < < < Aggressive

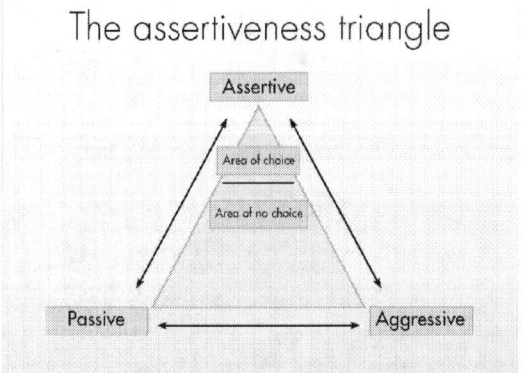

The assertiveness triangle

People who tend to be passive in interactions, do so for several reasons; because they:

- are shy,

- have low self-esteem,

- lack confidence,

- are socially inexperienced,

- are introverts,

- are submissive, and

- have weak personal boundaries.

Passive communicators do not defend their own boundaries. The problem with being passive is that:

(a) You can get pushed around
   (*viz.* manipulated, abused, badly treated).

(b) You do not state you feelings, thoughts and opinions
   (*i.e.* you supress everything).

(c) You become the "follower" too much of the time, allowing others to take responsibility
   (*viz.* in every situation you are never the leader or decision-maker).

The other extreme is being aggressive. These people are seen as heavy-handed and disrespectful of the personal boundaries of others. They have few friends and many enemies. Techniques this type of person uses, include:

- force,

- bossiness,

- demandingness,

- manipulation,

- threats, and

- violence.

Passive folk are the submissive types; by contrast, aggressors can be domineering, which means they are determined to control social situations and the people in them. You must not be seen as domineering or controlling, hence you must take care lest you monopolise the conversation, preventing others from talking as well.

Characteristics of Communication Styles

	Passive	Aggressive	Passive-Aggressive	Assertive
Active toward reaching one's goal?	No, ineffective strategy	Yes, but at the expense of others	Yes, but usually too late and inappropriately	Yes, and appropriately
Respectful?	Communicates apathy or submissiveness	No, intentions are to hurt others	No, mostly blame and guilt trips	Yes, even when defending their own safety
Listens to Others?	Maybe, but does not actively respond	Probably more concerned with own perspective	Maybe, but with hidden intentions	Yes, then responds at the appropriate time
Communicates Confidence?	No	Yes, probably too much	Maybe when acting aggressive	Yes, to set appropriate boundaries.
Uses Nonverbal Communication?	Yes, displays weakness and vulnerability	Yes, from threat gestures to injuring others	Yes, used to manipulate others	Yes, to reinforce appropriate verbal communication
Impression given to others?	Weakness, apathy	"Jerk" "Mean" you get the idea	Difficult to read, unpredictable	Easy to get along with, confident, cooperative
Reinforced by achievement of goals?	Yes, temporarily, if goal is to avoid conflict	Yes, immediate gratification, poor long term outcome	Yes, at the expense of relationships	Yes, and improves relationships
Examples of verbal interaction	I don't care Whatever Silent	F*@% You! I'll Kill You! You're Stupid!	It's your fault You should have... Sarcasm	"I" Statements When is a good time to talk?

Empathy and receptiveness

Being receptive and empathising with others are two of the most important communication skills. This means being sensitive to others' feelings and listening attentively and respectfully to what other people have to say, which shows at least that you are interested. In this you will be considering the rights, wants, needs, and personal boundaries of other people as well as your own.

You must also:

- encourage people to state their views and opinions, openly and honestly.

- show that you appreciate what they are saying, *e.g.* telling them, "I like that about you".

- make constructive comments, in lieu of negative ones.

- use appropriate questions to find out others' thoughts, views, and preferences.

Taking risks

We all tend to avoid taking risks in conversation and in any social situation; no one wants to "rock the boat". The problem with this strategy, though, is that we end up being the follower. Moreover, when we stick to a predefined script, we stay in our comfort zone and never grow.

We have to discipline ourselves to quit being risk averse: we cannot influence and persuade others without taking risks.

Barriers to assertiveness

All the barriers keeping us from being assertive lie within oneself. We project these mental barriers outwards and this becomes our reality.

The greatest barrier is our anxiety and fear about expressing ourselves fully, but here are other factors preventing us from being assertive, including:

- being too polite;
  i.e. we do not want to offend others,

- observing cultural and social differences;
  e.g. respect for elders,

- thinking that we do not have a right;
  i.e. we think we are the ones who are wrong,

- assuming that we might get ourselves alienated,

- lack of skills and/or experience, and

- feeling awkward and uncomfortable.

Beliefs about being assertive

The worst mistaken belief people have about being assertive is that other people will react adversely to them; *i.e.* they are afraid of what other people will think.

People stay passive to avoid giving offense or hurting people's feeling, and because they want to be liked and accepted. In effect, most of us are "people-pleasers". No matter what you say or which way you turn, there will always be some people who like you and some who don't. So, it is always best to choose the way of growth.

Here are some of the negative thoughts that might go through your mind to discourage your being assertive:

"What will people think of me?"

"I might look strange!"

"I don't want to make a scene."

"Who am I to go around imposing my opinion?"

"If I say whatever I want, people will be put off."

"I can't stand it when people get angry or upset with me."

Real life example

I now wish to highlight how assertiveness training can be used in social settings:

I was once invited to the grand opening party of a new restaurant by my friend James, the host. I attended the event with a few of my friends. The problem with the seating arrangement was that, although we were all part of the same social group, two sub-groups formed from time to time – the host and his friends *vs.* me and my friends, as diagrammed below.

This arrangement was acceptable for a while; however, I began to feel that there was an "invisible wall" separating us from them, as if each group was ignoring the other. Also, it prevented me from talking with the host's friends, whom I had never met before.

Host   Host's friend

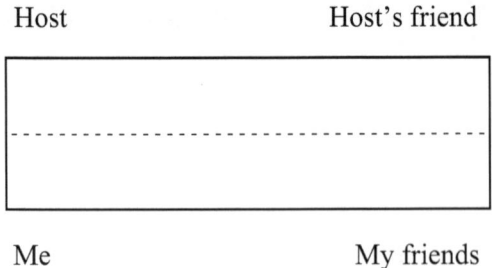

Me   My friends

So, I decided it was time to break through this wall, as my friends were evidently not willing to do so. I looked at one of the host's friends and said in a sharp tone, "What is your name?" She replied, "Jane". That small thing broke the "spell", and from that moment on, we were able to converse with the people across the table with ease.

Note, that at no point did I hesitate to interrupt the other people's conversation: because I was being assertive, I got the attention of them all, and I also knew what to say to follow up the introduction.

Lessons

- Never be afraid of anyone!

- Never be afraid of stating your case, in a conversation.

- Be fair but firm.

- Be unapologetic.

HIGH ASSERTIVENESS

Firm handshake.
Eye contact constant.
A lot of verbal communication.
Questions will challenge information, make points.
Firm statements of direction and thought.
Body gestures to emphasise communications.
Voice volume can be high.
Quick speed of words.
Voice emphasis with emotion.
Easily communicates.
Fast moving.

LOW ASSERTIVENESS

Softer handshake.
Intermittent eye contact.
Less verbal communications.
Questions are for support, information gathering,
clarification.
Very tentative in statements.
Body gestures are few and conservative (close to body).
Voice more reserved.
Words are measured and slow coming out.
Voice has little variation.
Communicates hesitantly.
Slow moving.

20. How to speak with passion in a conversation

"You mentioned (paraphrased): that you can talk about almost anything with passion and can be passionate about anything. Could you please expand on this? I know I have been passionate about things in the past but it's a bit hit and miss" **A. Student**

The word passion can have many meanings, and you can be passionate about many different things; for example:

- passionate about life,

- passionate about world peace, or

- passionate about a hobby.

Living in London for over 25 years, I have met people from every country of the world, of all ages from 16 to 60. I must admit that it is rare for me to meet someone who speaks with passion. At best, I would say most people's conversational skills are "dry" and their conversation verges on boring.

When we think of "passionate" speakers, we think of high profile leaders like Bill Clinton or Tony Robbins. We might not agree with everything they say, but we get absorbed in their conversation none the less. What makes these people stand out is that they were trained in public speaking, unlike the rest us. They use this training to magnetise and lead crowds of people.

Public speaking

Public speaking is all about engaging an audience. You are one person speaking to many people, thus it is a one-to-many interaction. This is never going to be an easy task, because you will never be able to please everyone or to hold everyone's attention span for long. You only have to look around as you speak and you will see people – yawning, staring into space, looking at their watches or mobile, chatting to friends, *etc.*

The skills you learn from public speaking can be applied to great advantage even when you are only talking to one person. When you are taught public speaking you learn many communication skills, including:

- making eye contact,

- maintaining positive body language,

- speaking in a sharp and loud voice tone,

- understanding the subject matter thoroughly,

- explaining topics well,

- keeping anxiety under control,

- making use of different delivery styles,

- being "present", and

- showing confidence.

Most people are already familiar with at least some of these considerations. The main question that is posed, however, is how we are supposed to transfer this skill-set to a social setting?

When I am talking about a social setting, I am referring to talking to a person (or a small group of people).

One-to-one

A one-to-one conversation is much easier to manage than a one-to-many conversation.

You are advantaged in this type of setting in many ways; for example:

- you can get undivided attention from the listener,

- you are able to form a deep connection with him/her,

- you can empathise with each other, and

- experiences can be shared back and forth.

So, a one-to-one conversation is a two-way communication process, unlike with public speaking.

Having a passion

Having a passion is not the same thing as speaking with passion: it does not equate to a person being able to communicate with passion.

Plenty of people you meet every day are passionate about what they do at work or play, but when they speak to you about the subject, it is usually not absorbing, unfortunately.

One reason for this, as mentioned above, is that they have not been trained in how to speak. There are other reasons, too, which will be mentioned below.

Expression not impression

The first lesson you must learn to become an effective conversationalist is to be yourself. Be honest. Be genuine. Be your authentic self when you communicate

Most people are not comfortable with revealing themselves to others whom they have just met; this is what I call the "stranger complex". It will be your task to learn to relax and let go of yourself.

A one-to-one conversation is an intimate affair compared to public speaking. You must not be afraid of "revealing all your cards". You have to take the initiative in opening up, then the other person will follow.

Note also that, women tend to say (with disappointment) that men do not sufficiently reveal or express their feelings or emotions.

EASE HAPPY OR AMUSED LAUGHTER

ANGER HATE AGGRESSIVE

SAD BORED MILD

DMV30221

Conversation content

The content of what you say does matters!

It is well known that the salience of logical content in communication is estimated to be around 10% to 20%, but this seemingly small percentage cannot be ignored.

Some people claim that you can "say anything" in a conversation and it does not matter. I disagree with this statement profoundly; I am constantly seeking to develop the content of my conversation, knowing from experience that this will improve my communication skills in all settings.

If you do not have the right content when speaking to a person, you are likely to come across as:

- boring,

- one dimensional, and

- lacking personality.

To improve you conversational content, you must include these key elements:

(a) **Interesting topics**
Look for unusual subjects and be creative and imaginative.

Talk about things that others may not be aware of or have never heard of before.

(b) **Depth in the material**
It is inadequate to skim over your material or to be superficial in conversation.

You need to research your topics of conversation.

(c) **Mixing and matching**
Do not spend hours taking about the same topic in the same way.

When talking about different subjects, use different tools (*e.g.* humour, cold-readings)

Material for conversation is all around you at all times. You need not search high and low to find topics worth talking about. It would behove you to get into the habit of turning the ordinary into the extraordinary!

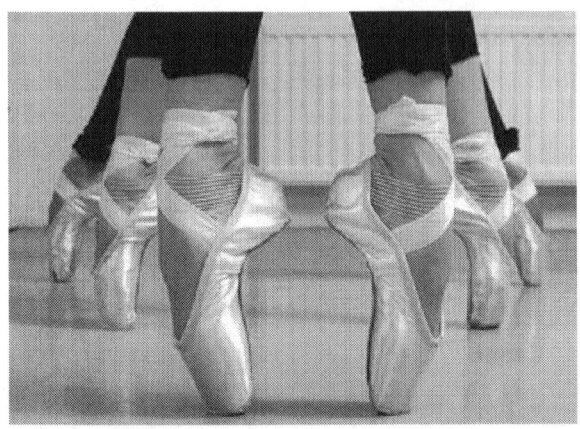

Emotions are contagious

Passion is all important in conversation.

Passion underlies motivation, and this in turn leads us on to action. When we feel passionate about a matter, we are likely to do something about it. The converse of this, of course, is also true.

- Is your heart in it?

- Is it for real?

- Or, are you just going through the motions?

It is often remarked that artists are passionate about their art. We should approach the things of life in the same spirit. If you are doing thing mechanically, you will become a "robot of routines".

In this condition you are unable to empathise with people in your social circle.

There are three other important emotions closely related to passion; they are:

- enthusiasm,

- excitement, and

- eagerness.

All three go hand-in-hand: if you are passionate about something, you will also be excited, eager and enthusiastic about it.

Energy

All the three emotional states have a unique energy about them. This energy "radiates" outwards, so that people listening to you will be and attracted and absorbed into the topic, and also into you who are expounding it.

Body language and intensity

I have noticed that when I am talking about a subject I am passionate about, my body language will change in a way peculiar to me (everyone will undergo their own change). This change follows a set order:

1. My hands come together in front of me as if I am about to grip something.

2. My head bends downwards to look towards the spherical gap in my hands.

3. My voice slows down.

There is an intense feeling that comes over me as I "cycle" through this behavioural process, both before and during my talk. I am totally absorbed in what I say. I tend to forget myself before the person in front of me as I get absorbed as if into another world.

The process was internalised long ago; I do not have to think about being passionate. I just speak in this manner as if on "auto-pilot".

In the zone

When athletes and sportsmen behave this way, they are said to be "in the zone".

When talking about a subject I am passionate about, I am totally in the zone; I forget myself in the midst of the things and people around me. I also am not aware of time slipping by.

Lessons

Speak with passion in your conversation.

Communication is about content and energy. The energy you exude will attract people toward you and toward what you are saying.

You will get people's full attention at this stage, and they will want to have and enjoy some of what you have!

PASSION

I'm A Firm Believer In The Theory That People Only
Do Their Best At Things They Truly Enjoy. It Is
Difficult To Excel At Something You Don't Enjoy.
~ Jack Nicklaus ~

Compliments of The People's Cyber Nation - http://www.cyber-nation.com. ©1997 Cyber Nation International, Inc.

21. Do not anticipate

How many times have we worried ourselves with thoughts like the following?

"What does he think of me?"

"Do they like me?"

"How can I please them?"

"Did I offend him?"

"How can I get her to like me?"

"How can I get him to stay with me in a relationship?"

These are some of the thoughts that kill passion. We become too much absorbed in these worries and in ourselves when we try too hard to relate to another person.

Uncertain world

Human beings crave certainty.

We live in a world where certainty does not exist, however, and unfortunately, we often make the mistake of trying to impose certainty by an act of will. If we do not know the answer to something, we make the answer up, anticipating what the other person will do, say, think or feel. It is like trying to assemble the pieces of a large, complex jigsaw puzzle.

Along with certainty we all crave stability and security, sometimes referred to as "permanence".

If we have something we want today, then we want it to be there tomorrow. The prime example of this is a relationship with someone you love. Couples in relationships tend to worry themselves with questions like:

"Will he still love me tomorrow?"

"What happens if she finds another man?"

"Will I be able to cope with being single again?"

Negative psychic predictions

In our quest for certainty, we typically try to predict things in advance of the event. Unfortunately, most of these predictions tend to be negative and will not serve our purpose.

We are always dreaming up worst-case scenarios, obsessing over thoughts like:

"What if things go wrong?"

"What if they reject me?

"What if I look stupid?"

Needless to say, all this leads to worry, anxiety and stress. We must learn how to stay clear of these negative thoughts.

Pie Chart of My Daily Thoughts
(My Wife)

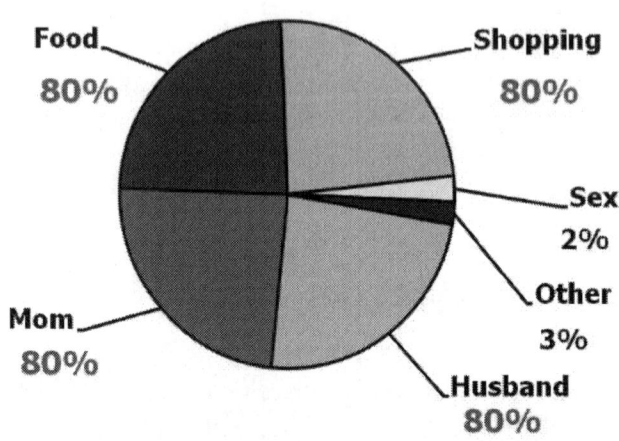

Food
80%

Shopping
80%

Sex
2%

Other
3%

Mom
80%

Husband
80%

Mind reading others

We will never really know what other people are thinking about.

We will never know what "state of mind" other people are in.

We will never fully understand why people behave the way they do.

We will never be sure where other people are coming from.

We will never be able to step into other peoples shoes.

We must accept the fact that it is essentially impossible to understand how our own minds work, let alone understand the workings of other people's minds. Mind reading is a risky, futile exercise.

We may convince ourselves that we know what others are thinking about, but most of the time our assumptions are wrong. Indeed, another person may not be thinking about you at all while you are furiously calculating that they think of you.

*"We spend our time thinking about what other people are thinking about us...when all they're really thinking about is what we're thinking about them." **Ellen DeGeneres***

Anticipation, all over again

When meeting people for the first time, you will have little knowledge or information about them, so, do not anticipate by:

- Guessing their thoughts.

- Predicting their actions and behaviours.

- Pre-empting what they are going to say next.

- Trying to fathom their emotions and feelings.

Lesson

Stop!! mind-reading other people.

22. Do not make assumptions

"Don't assume anything!"

This is the phrase you hear people saying all the time.

An assumption is a thought or belief the correctness of which we do not pause to question, though we have no evidence to back it up. In effect, we are extrapolating or predicting things based on our past experiences. Assumptions are mainly about other people, relationship issues in particular, and usually negative. For example, we may assume our girlfriend is seeing another man or that our boss is planning to sack us.

Start with a blank slate

In reality, every moment of our life is like a new starting point.

Every situation we encounter and every person who enters our life should be regarded as a blank slate. Anything we do to colour it is based on our perceptions. We project our perceptions outwards onto people and things around us. Most of the time, we see what we want to see and hear what we want to hear.

These projections are typically based on our fears and insecurities and/or on our anxious need to control people and situations, as we are constantly seeking clarity and certainty in our lives.

Making up meanings

Nothing around us has any inherent meaning in itself.

We add meaning to the things around us by way of our thinking process. Although meaning is indeed socially constructed, it is still to a significant degree individually subjective, as no two people think alike, and different people will interpret the same situation differently.

We have a tendency to impute meaning even where none exists; for example, seeing your girlfriend having coffee with another man, you become suspicious and impute unfaithfulness. Thus we give meaning to a situation irrespective of its truth. In our mind we feel compelled to fill in the blanks and complete the story or picture; we cannot accept leaving the matter unresolved and uncertain.

The drive for meaning overrides any preference we might have for logical reasoning, and yet we say ourselves that other people "jump to conclusions" too quickly.

Our senses can lie

Relying on your senses for information can be tricky. In ages past, people used to think the earth was flat, because such was the evidence of their senses.

Our senses give us part of the picture but not the whole. When we discover that this is so, we are tempted to complete the picture by making assumptions, as that is easier than taking the trouble to investigate.

If we would communicate more effectively, we must resist making assumptions, and instead find out or investigate things in greater depth.

Clarity in conversation

Communication with other people will be flawed if we make assumptions instead of understanding the situation. This leads directly to misunderstanding, for example if we assume someone does not like us or will reject us. It is more in your own interest to know where they are coming from and be able to empathise.

Follow these guidelines to open up better communication with other people and to avoid making assumptions:

- Listen carefully to what the other person is saying.

- Be in the moment and give them your full attention.

- Ask question if you are not sure about something.

- Be patient and give everyone a chance to speak.

- Do not interrupt the speaker and avoid jumping in.

- Think before you speak by reflecting on what the other person has said.

- Summarise or rephrase what they have told you.

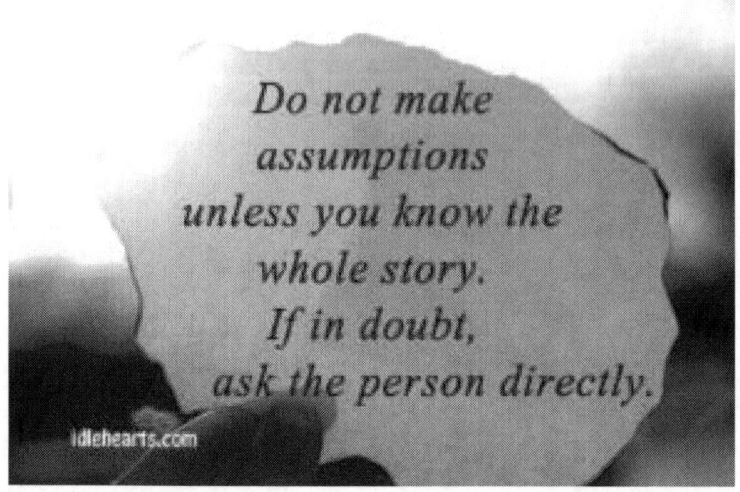

Avoid creating "what if?" fantasies

Making assumptions can be a dangerous thing!

To make an assumption is, to assume we know the truth. Most of our assumptions are based on little or no facts or evidence.

We make assumptions about others by relating them to ourselves, even if they are not thinking about us; *viz.*:

(a) **"What are they thinking?"**
(*i.e.* they think badly of me)

(b) **"What is he doing?"**
(*i.e.* they are plotting something against me)

(c) **"What is she feeling?"**
  (*i.e.* she hates me)

Starting with such assumptions, we go on to create "what if?" scenarios in our heads.

What is she thinking?

We habitually think about what our partners and other people we love are thinking about. This is a futile exercise; it is complicated enough to understand our own minds, let alone the minds of others.

When you think about what she is thinking about, then all you are doing is making assumptions.

When you think about what she will do or say next, then all you are doing is making assumptions.

Stop thinking and worrying about what other people are thinking or doing.

"What is he thinking?" "What does he think of me?"
"Will he like me?" "Am I his type?" "Is he single?"

23. Do not seek approval

(*a.k.a.* validation seeking)

"Care about people's approval and you will be their prisoner" **Lao Tzu**

"Will they approve of me or not?"

"Will they like me or not?"

"Will they accept me or not?"

We constantly seek the approval of others, and fear their disapproval.

Approval-seeking is an automatic behaviour that has been programmed in us from youth. If we are always having to check-in with others before we act, then we have surrendered ourselves to them.

We compulsively put others before ourselves, by checking with them first through a thought process something like this:

> We all think about doing something > > > Then we think about how people will respond to me > > > We do the deed > > > We look to see how people react > > > People react positively or not > > > Then we react to their reactions. Thereby, their reactions control us.

Social conditioning in childhood

We learn to seek approval from others at a young age. As children we depend on adults for our survival. The consequent conditioning goes on at all times: in school, at home and on the job (if we have one). There is a clear reward and punishment system that underpins this conditioning: if you do as you are told, you get rewarded; if not, you are punished.

Being naïve and innocent in our youth, we look to our elders for guidance. In behavioural terms, we work to get their approval and the rewards that follow. This pattern of conditioning carries on in the workplace and other spheres of adult life.

Peer pressure is also a conditioning towards conformism. It happens whenever we strive to please not only our friends but everyone else in our social circle. This affects all our social activities from our dress to our tastes in music, and on and on.

People pleasers (a.k.a. approval junkies)

It is necessary to seek approval when we are young, but part of growing up is reassessing the system of social conditioning.

Being compliant with others' wishes render us submissive and too easily exploited.

Having to live up to expectations and please others at all times, robs us of our power and freedom. We are beholden to others and unable to do what we want.

Other people's moods and emotions are constantly changing, and a people-pleaser must constantly abnegate herself in adjusting to their whims, sometimes even without realising it. In effect, you give up your identity and become a "clone", like others who are doing exactly the same thing.

Behaviour

We put ourselves under pressure if we feel we have to act and say things just to get people's approval. In many cases, we have to figure out first whether they will like what we do or say before we do or say it.

People who are seeking approval will typically do things like:

- show off their achievements.

- tell lies.

- tell people what they want to hear.

We are constantly worrying that people will disapprove of us if we do not do whatever they want.

Acceptance from others

People-pleasers feel elated if they get something as trifling as a nod of approval from others and feel sad if they do not. We link our emotional state, our self-esteem and our identity to that approval, so that we react emotionally to people who express their disapproval of us. This is the proof that we are approval junkies.

> *"The average man is too concerned with liking people or with being liked himself. A warrior likes, that's all. He likes whatever or whomever he wants, for the hell of it."*
> **Carlos Castaneda**

Expression not impression

We can teach ourselves to avoid trying to impress people, to get them to like us. What we must do instead is freely express ourselves in all our thoughts, words and deeds. The key is to break the habit of filtering or censoring everything we say and do, trying to guess what will please others.

Stop the chatter in your head

We can discipline ourselves positively to shut down the self-talk in our heads that is dependent upon the approval of others, such as:

"Did she like me?"

"Will she want to see me again?"

"What will they think of me?"

"Did I come across as stupid?"

"Why did they not find me funny?"

After a conversation or meeting, such chatter leads to more self-talk like:

"I should have said ..."

"I could have done ..."

"I should have said ... to her."

"I should never have said that."

"I should have worn my new skirt."

All that life requires of you is to do your best and then leave things as they are, without the endless self-talk which only reinforces our need for approval.

Do not judge

We spend much time judging people, places and things around us. Our judgements are all reflections on ourselves, not others. Judging includes things like:

- criticising,

- complaining,

- negativity,

- blaming,

- stereotyping,

- condemning,

- abusing, and

- swearing.

"You hypocrite, first take the log out of your own eye, and then you will see clearly to take the speck out of your brother's eye." **Matthew 7:5**

We are constantly judging other people and they are constantly doing the same to us. We are all very critical of other people, even if we know nothing about them. We are afraid to be ourselves and express ourselves around others knowing they will judge us the same way we judge them.

By assuming other people will judge us harshly or reject us, we reject ourselves even before we get a chance to meet or talk to the other person.

"We have learned to live our lives trying to satisfy other people's demands. We have learned to live by other people's points of view because of the fear of not being accepted and of not being good enough for someone else."
D M Ruiz

Lessons

- Seeking approval from others is a futile exercise that must be stopped.

- Judging people on appearances must be stopped.

- The only person you must get approval from is yourself – this is self-approval.

- Let go of needing other people's approval.

24. Do not take anything personally

Your opinions are your opinions and my opinions are mine!

I do not value your opinions of me, be they good or bad, more that I value my opinions of myself.

Avoid linking your identity or sense of self to the opinions of others.

It is not other people's opinions that get you down, but how you react to them.

Social conditioning from childhood

From a very young age we become sensitive to the opinions of others, especially the ones who mean the most to us. At home our parents tell us that we are behaving or not. At school teachers tell us that we are succeeding or not. At the workplace, our supervisors tell us that we are performing well or not. If we are religious, then our pastors will tell us that we are good or bad people.

We react emotionally, taking personally other people's evaluations of us thanks to the years of being conditioned by the judgements of significant others. It is because of the emotional reaction that we end up believing implicitly that their judgements about us must be true.

My identity is for me to decide

Throughout our most formative years we link our identity to whatever other people say about us. In other word, we become "externally referenced". If something good is said about use, we feel great but if something bad is said, we feel discouraged. We become obsessed with wanting people to view us always in a favourable light.

We give too much weight to the opinions of others, assuming that, it is important what they think about us.

Concerning your identity and self-esteem, realise that what you think of yourself is rather of utmost importance. In this, modesty is the best policy. Pride cannot be sustained without the approval of others, whereas modesty is sustainable and requires much less validation.

Letting go

Taking thing personally implies that:

- we identify with, and

- indeed have blind faith in

other people's word as being the fact and the truth about ourselves.

You become independent of the judgement of others by letting go of the pleasure you take in their praise; in this way their blame does not matter so much anymore. You can also avoid emotionalism by stopping your obsessively rehearsing in your head their actual or anticipated judgements. Then only will other people's opinions have little effect on you.

Your opinions are a reflection of yourself

Other people's opinions are about them and not about you!

Their opinions really have nothing to do with who you really are.

Everything you think, say and do is a product of your internal beliefs and values. Whenever, we pass judgment on others or pronounce our opinion of them, it all comes from our own subjective reality.

You need to carve out a life of your own by taking responsibility for making your own decisions. You have to place full trust in yourself, not in others.

CONFESSION #548 ...

I Don't Try To Get Other People To Approve Of Me

What they think of me is none of my business,
BUT what I think about myself is everything.

500confessions.com

Lessons

No matter what people do, feel, think or say about you, don't take it personally.

Believe in yourself and trust your own choices.

25. Body language and sub-communication

Our communication is transmitted through two main channels:

- verbal communication constitutes only about 1/3 of the meaning that gets transmitted, but

- non-verbal communication constitutes fully 2/3 of the meaning.

Thus, non-verbal communication (NVC) is the medium of most of our communication. Non-verbal communication is transmitted via body language and voice tone, and the rest is sub-communicated; *viz.* being relaxed or confident, being nervous or anxious.

Body language refers to such outer-game components as:

- eye contact,

- smiling or frowning,

- other facial expressions,

- comporting yourself in the presence others,

- placement of your hands,

- posture,

- gestures,

- how you sit down;
  e.g. taking up space when sitting.

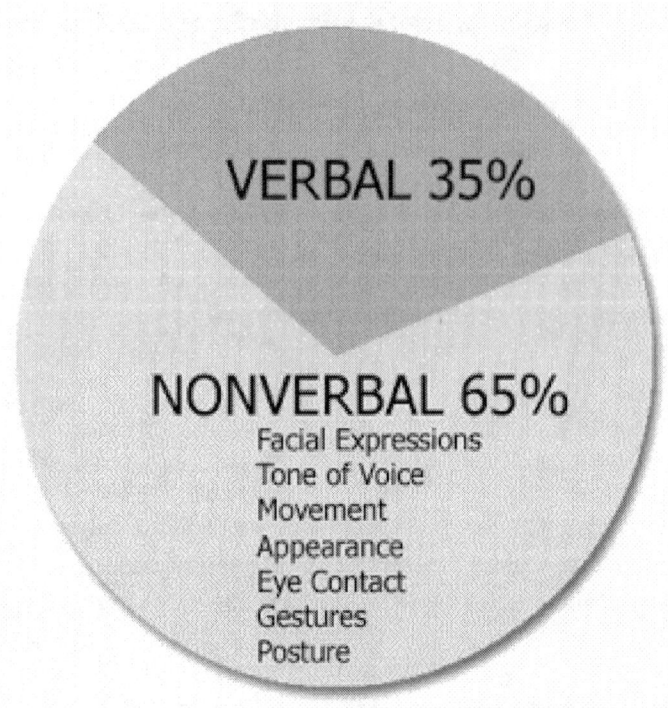

VERBAL 35%

NONVERBAL 65%
Facial Expressions
Tone of Voice
Movement
Appearance
Eye Contact
Gestures
Posture

People-readers

People are constantly reading each other in social situations.
Whether we are aware of it or not, we are "people-readers" for
much the same reasons we are people-pleasers. Constantly
"transmitting" our inner state to those around us, simultaneously
we are reading (or "receiving") their state. People are acutely
aware of whether your current state is positive or negative.

Being aware that others are constantly forming opinions of us by
the way we come across, we feel obliged to make the first best
impression by putting our best selves forward.

We also have to be aware of the signals people around us are "broadcasting". You need to practice becoming aware of these signals and learn how to read them.

Cultivate your body language and always be on the lookout for ways to improve it.

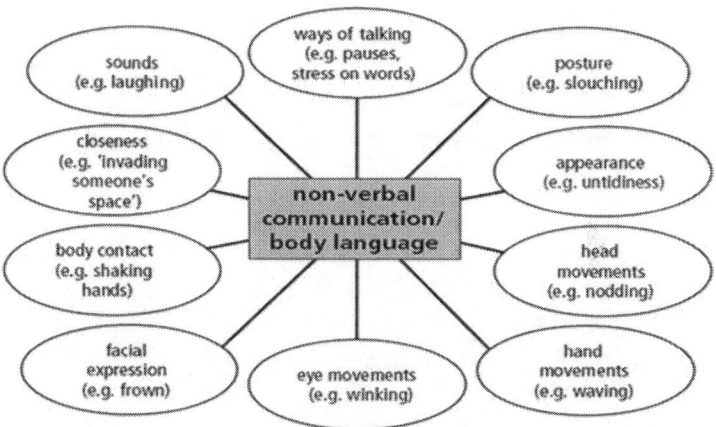

Lie detectors and emotional leakages

The term "leakages" refers to the emotions, usually negative, which we try to conceal, but which can be unconsciously sub-communicated nonetheless via body language. When our verbal communication contradicts our sub-communication, this is leakage. A classic example is when a criminal perpetrator tries to convince the police he is innocent. He insists on his innocence in vain, whose body language conveys nervousness, as if he had something to hide. Law enforcement and interrogation specialists are trained in reading body language.

In social situations, we often feel we can get away with telling "little white lies" and using deception. For example, we may brag that we have visited a country we have never been to, or claim we own a big house or expensive car when we do not. Most people are able to detect signs of leakage, no matter how hard the speaker tries to hide it.

First impressions are pivotal to subsequent social relationships; any lie that is detected can taint the entire perception a person has about you; therefore, always aim to be authentic and honest in all of your conversations.

This book will not explain body language in detail, as too many very good books have already been written on this subject.

26. Identity and values: how are you defined?

Your identity consists of the distinguishing factors that make you the person you are. Given that we are unique, your identity is personal and individual to you. It includes your character, personality, behaviour, attitudes, qualities, values, *etc.*

The two most important points about your identity is that it must be:

- authentic, and

- strong.

All the stories you tell about yourself go into the formation of your identity. There are many aspects to identity. One way of looking at it is by making a list of the 10 things you are most interested in and passionate about; for example, for me this list includes:

1. Travel.

2. Dance.

3. Food and nutrition.

4. Business and entrepreneurship.

5. Animals.

6. Social and emotional intelligence, relationships.

7. Meditation, spirituality, yoga.

8. Movies and music.

9.   Acting and Stand-up Comedy.

10. Art.

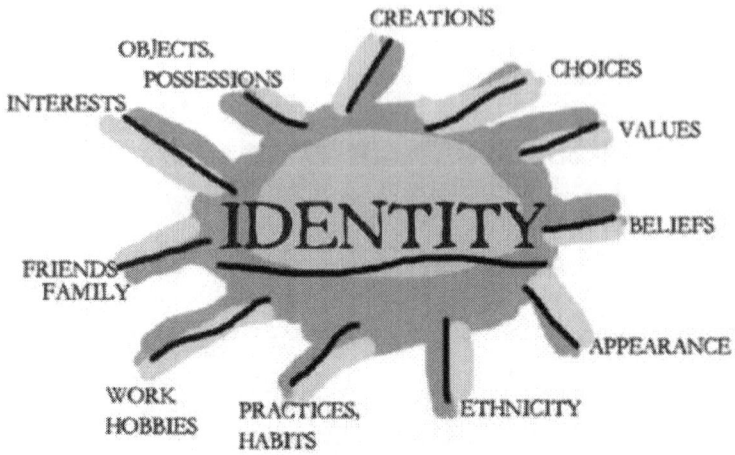

Values

Values are those governing principles in life that you count as worthy in themselves and believe you ought to live by. Values are:

(a) **Intrinsic**

(*i.e.* they are not external items like wealth or possessions); and

(b) **Intangible**

(*e.g.* you cannot touch or see them).

It is of the essence of happiness that your values align with your passions, life purpose, beliefs, goals and identity; thus, if you care about the environment, you need to do something about it personally.

Some values we take for granted, yet recognise as essential for life to run smoothly. Examples of these include: freedom, friendship, generosity, kindness, forgiveness.

Values guide our decision and determine our motivations. Examples of this include common values like: abundance, choice, growth, honesty, independence, integrity, passion, respect, trust.

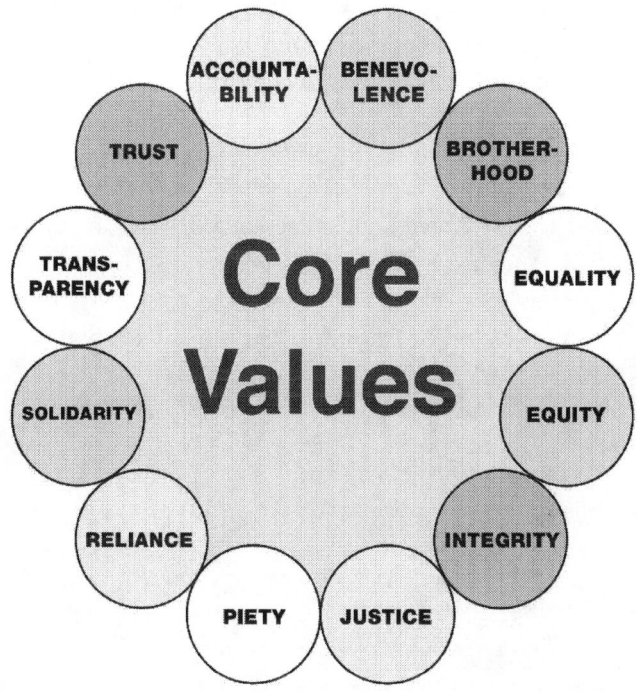

Eliciting underlying values

We cannot know values by our senses, as they are all intangible; however, we are aware of our need for them, and tend to show discontent in their absence.

There are values that most of us take for granted, but see as being essential for things to run smoothly. Examples of these values include freedom, friendship, generosity, kindness, forgiveness.

When we meet people for the first time, we get to know them at a preliminary level by learning their likes and dislikes, *e.g.* what they do for a living or their hobbies and interests.

People are attracted to these things because they satisfy certain underlying values that matter to them; for example, the student who takes a year off to volunteer for a charity overseas is likely to hold values of giving, compassion and adventure.

People do not rattle off their values to others, as they may not be aware of them: their values lie at a deeper level of their persona. This means you will have to do some "digging" to find them out, without asking them direct questions about the information you are looking for.

When eliciting another person's values, you need to look for their:

(a) **Hobbies and interests**
ask them:

> "What do you like to do in your free time?"

> "Do you do it a lot?"

(*e.g.* if they do a lot of travelling, then adventure may be one of their values; if they go in for sports, then one value is probably fitness).

(b) **Work and profession**

> "What aspect of your work do you like?"

> "Do you like to do things that you are not able to do?

(*e.g.* if they are a nurse, one of their values is bound to be caring; if they run their own business, then one value is surely independence).

(c) **Ambitions and aspirations**
To elicit underlying values, you can ask questions along the lines of:

"What would your ideal vacation be like?"

"In which country would you like to live?

"What would you like to become, if it could be anything?"

(this is an indication of their drives, desires and motivations for the future)

27. Setting a friendly frame: assume familiarity

If you act like a stranger around people, then they will treat you like a stranger.

Conversely, if you treat a person like a stranger, then they will then behave like a stranger.

Whenever we are around friends we tend to be relaxed and comfortable with what we say and do. By contrast, when we are talking to people we have only just met, we tend to "keep our distance". This is what I call the "stranger complex". Now, what if we could "assume familiarity" with those we have just met, treating them like an old friend?

Body language

Just by glancing around, we can immediately tell if a group of people, say in a bar or club, are friends with each other or not. Those who are getting to know each other and are only recently acquainted will exhibit body language like the following:

- **Keeping their distance**
  i.e. so as not to invade others' personal space.

- **Positioning themselves to face the other person**
  i.e. they are not casual enough to face in a less "respectful" directions.

- **Showing animated body language**
  i.e. they are trying to impress their new acquaintances.

- **Looking tense and uncertain at times**
  i.e. they are not all that relaxed and comfortable.

- **Not smiling**
  i.e. they look serious because they feel that way.

- **Seeming somewhat shy or reserved**
  i.e. they are still building up their confidence.

Attraction and connection

Assuming familiarity from the start in such circumstances is an attraction trigger: it shows that the assumer has confidence and social intelligence. By contrast, the "stranger complex" delays attraction and connection, which cannot begin to happen until the people involved are feeling comfortable both with themselves and with each other. Hence, the importance of learning how to relax and wind down your energy soon after you meet someone for the first time.

It will be your duty to relax and to get other people to do the same.

To help in assuming familiarity, you can ask yourself the question, "How would I act around this person if he was a life-long friend?" When you are hanging out with friends you would more likely:

- pace the conversation slowly and steadily.

- pause for reflection.

- look away distracted from time-to-time.

- point to something (*e.g.* people, rooms, drinks) to call her attention to it; creating a "shared moment" between just the two of you.

A typical conversation you would have with a friend at a new venue might include:

- describing to them what the red VIP room in the corner is like.

- asking them, "What do you think of the people/the bar/the music?"

- telling them how your day or week went by.

- talking about your other friends and family.

At what point in the interaction will the person you have just met progress from being a stranger to being a friend? This very much depends on you, and more importantly on your mind-set.

Communications Triangle

In the pyramidal diagram, the base represents small talk while the peak represents deep connection. In order to move up, we have to reveal more of ourselves; it also means that they will have to do the same. This process can be conducted as follows:

(a) **Start assuming familiarity as soon as possible**
   i.e. spend as little time as possible on small talk.

(b) **Progress gradually**
   If you over-do it early on, it could lead the other person to think:

   "Why is he telling me so much about himself?"

If you are still unsure how to assume familiarity, ask yourself these two questions:

   "How do I act when I am with my friends?"

   "How do I talk (or say things) when I am around my friends?"

28. Goal setting: having a Game Plan

Planning and implementation is as important a part of improving our conversation skill-set, as it is in other aspects of our lives. To facilitate this, you should keep a log or journal of your conversations and other social interactions.

Importance of a Game Plan

The Game Plan answers three fundamental questions with three fundamental "P's":

1. What are we going to do?	the Planning
2. How are we going to do it?	the Practice (or implementation)
3. When are we going to do it?	the Progress

Without answering these three questions, we will not have structure or a framework to work within.

Key points about a Game Plan

Key to a successful Game Plan is that you:

- Make it part of your learning and training programme.

- Use it to monitor your progress and achievements.

- Be specific with what you write in it, as this will help you with the implementation,
  i.e. avoid generality, vagueness or on the other hand too much detail, and not more than one page.

- Discuss it with your friends, before you go out.

- Take it with you to the social venue for reference.

- Make it fun to put into action and build-in flexibility,
  i.e. avoid being too rigid or routine.

- Update it regularly,
  e.g. every few weeks.

- Keep back copies to review or for future reference.

- Use your own material, so as to be authentic and express your core personality.

"Never leave home without one" ... a Game Plan, that is!

Below is a Game Plan template that you can fill in:

GAME PLAN – TEMPLATE [date]
No. of outings per week: 3 to 4
No. of people to approach per outing: 5 to 7

INNER GAME

- I socialise, have fun and am playful – I live in the moment.
- I am the party; I bring people into my party, I do not step into theirs.
- I am the most important person in the conversation.
- I will invest in all Interactions and add social value.
- I don't care what anyone thinks of me;
  I have 100% belief in myself.

START GAME

- Openers
- Transition

MID GAME

- 3 Stories
- 1 Cold-reading
- 1 Role-playing
- Humour/Teasing

END GAME

- Do I want to keep in touch with the other person?
- Will I get the other persons phone number?
- How can I meet up with this person again?

BASICS – REMINDER

- Body language,
  e.g. smile, make eye contact, take up space, slow down your gestures.
- Be a doer, not a watcher or mere listener.
- Be proactive: unreactive, "think outside my head"
  i.e. calm your inner chatter box.
- Have 100% confidence.

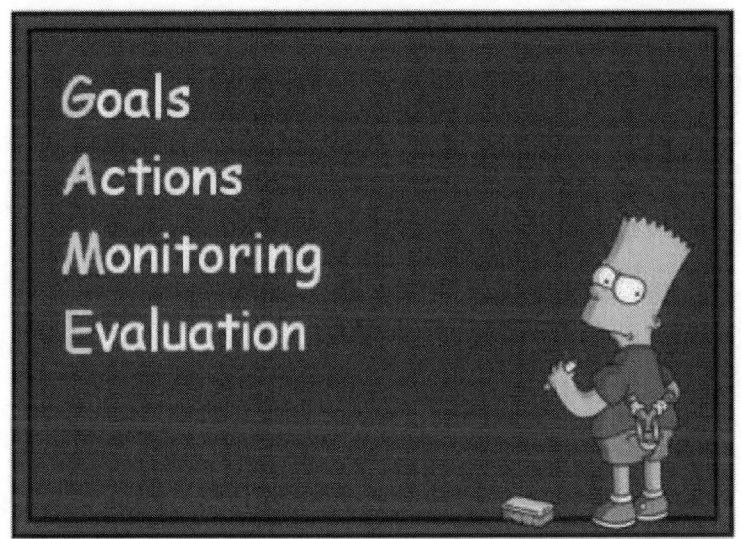

Exercises

Follow these steps and prepare a Game Plan for the coming week:

1. Write out a set of inner-game changes you want to work on.

2. Write out a list of "Basics – Reminders" you already know about.

3. Set a goal for how often you will go out and how many people you will approach.

4. Plan out one main opener and transition.

5. Write specific routines for the mid-game, *e.g.* stories, cold-readings, humour or teasing, role-playing, connection and rapport questions.

6. Prepare the Game Plan template, as above, and save it.

7. Rehearse the Game Plan by yourself or with a wingman.

8. Implement your Game Plan in the coming week.

9. Journal the events that take place in the field.

10. Use your current Game Plan to help you prepare a new one for the week following.

29. Handling criticism correctly

"It is not the situation that makes the man, but the man who makes the situation." **Frederick Robertson**

As we go about our daily lives meeting familiar and new people, some conflict and criticism from others is bound to arise from time to time. I would be surprised if I did not occasionally come across a critic, considering how many people I meet from around the world. The more experience you gain at conversation, the more you will have ventured outside your comfort zone, and you will have found that not everyone agrees with everything you say. Confidence in conversation is about not fearing anyone and saying exactly what you think; it is about being authentic.

The most important aspect about handling criticism is not so much what other people say, but how you react to them. The only thing you have control over is how you yourself think and react. You may be able to influence and persuade other people, but not to control them. You must always stay calm and centred; hence the importance of learning inner game. Never take personally anything another person says (see Chapter 24). People push your "hot buttons" sometimes deliberately and sometimes even when they are not aware of it. If you do not react, they will get the "message" that they cannot affect you that way.

What is criticism?

Criticism consists of other people's judgements on us; it is about their opinions, feeling and views, which may or may not accurately reflect on us, as people do make snap judgements. Criticism often tells us more about the critic than the criticised.

Moreover, even well-meaning, the critic may know may know much about us, or not know us well at all.

Criticism may be pejorative or negative comments or it may be constructive. How does one decide which is which? Firstly, keep an open mind and do not dismiss criticism just because you do not like it. Consider what they have said and, if need be, ask for clarification; for example:

> You: "I have travelled to Barcelona and I think it is an amazing place."
>
> Critic: "It's a dump!"
>
> You: "I am not sure what you mean – can you tell me about your experience?"

Asking clarifying questions gives you time to consider, evaluate and understand what the critic has said. This is what good conversation is about – it must be a two-way dialogue.

It is important to learn from constructive, positive criticism. As for the pejorative and negative, it is best to ignore it.

Modes of response

As just mentioned above, conversation is a two-way dialogue. There are several ways you can respond to the criticisms of others:

1. *Agreement*

This is the best course to take in the midst of a conversation, as it will always move it forward. It is also helpful to all if you state your reasons for agreeing with them. However, do not fall into the trap of agreeing with everything they say; then it becomes approval-seeking or supplication.

You can even agree with the critic's opinion, but disagree on a specific point relating to it; for example:

> Critic: "What exercises are you doing at the moment?"
>
> You: "None. I am working twelve hours every day. I get home, eat and then sleep."
>
> Critic: "That's nonsense! It's just an excuse. We all need to be doing exercise for about ten hours per week."
>
> You: "You know, you're probably right."

2. *Agreeing to disagree*

There will be many things we disagree upon when we are speaking to people. However, this need not necessarily create conflict. Firstly, you should always seek out agreement on some aspect of what the critic has said, rather than totally rejecting all of his remarks; for example:

> You: "People are eating too much meat in their diets."
>
> Critic: "That's nonsense! We should all have meat in our diets."
>
> You: "I can see where you are coming from. Our ancestors ate a mixed diet, and meat does contains essential proteins and other vitamins; however, I personally won't eat meat."

3. *Reasoned debate*

This is a "mini" or "heated" argument, but not a full-out war. You do not agree with everything they say but neither do you disagree with everything. You do need to be knowledgeable on the topic under discussion. You should make it clear why you agree and on what points you disagree, for example:

You: "People are eating too much meat in their diets."

Critic: "That's nonsense! We should all have meat in our diets."

You: "There are good reasons to eat meat because ... but research has also shown the negative consequences of an animal based diet because ..."

4. *Disengagement*

This is when you leave or withdraw from that particular conversation. It is not to be recommended generally, as the objective is to stay in the conversation as long as possible.

Staying in an interaction has several long term advantages; it can:

- develop your conversation skillset,

- improve your confidence,

- give you exposure to people from different backgrounds, and

- make you better at dealing with difficult people.

This option should only be used as a last resort.

5. Denial

You absolve yourself of all responsibility in this instance, by saying that it is not your problem, or it has nothing to do with you, or by downplaying its importance. This course of action can be chosen when sensitive topics are discussed like the environment, third world poverty, religion, morality, *etc.*

6. Counter attacking

This is hitting back with spite and vengeance. The critic will point out something you have done wrong or something you should improve upon; you take offence at his criticism and immediately you strike back; for example:

> Critic: "Why did you come to my party dressed like a tramp!?"

> You: "Look who's talking; I see you dressed like a slob all the time."

This becomes open warfare and is not conducive to conversation, and does not tackle the issues or problems at hand.

7. Defensiveness

This is when we put up a barrier against the criticism levelled at us. We remain sensitive to it but refuse to acknowledge it in any way. In this mode we do not listen and even tend to shut down our awareness of what is happening around us. There is no understanding of what the critic is saying. We may go so far as to defend our position when inappropriate or incorrect.

Defensiveness is an emotional reaction, and can take the form of making excuses, changing the subject, ignoring the remark, or refusing to discuss the matter.

A few rare instances exist when it is best to ignore criticism, and I will mention them below.

The several "flavours" of negative criticism

People will find different ways or resort to certain techniques to criticise you. Here are the main pejorative or negative criticisms that I have come across:

1. *Having a superiority complex*

The critic is just egotist and is trying to prove he is better that you. He may do so by bragging about how wealthy he is, how well connected he is, about how far he has travelled, *etc*. He may deliberately put you down.

2. *Being rude*

If the critic is outright offensive toward you, they could have a problem personality or bad temperament. They may ridicule you or say you don't know what you're talking about. If they only say one or two rude things, then it might be just a forgivable slip of the tongue.

3. *Being argumentative*

These people are domineering in life. They usually want to take control of the conversation and make it about themselves. They could do this by devaluing your opinions, challenging you about everything, or interrupting you. This turns the conversation into a monologue.

4. *Blame-gaming*

The critic could blame you for something you did or even for something that may be wholly unrelated to you. This is a personal attack on your character, in which case, you can ask the person for the evidence (assuming you are innocent). There could also be an element of jealousy involved.

The best way to deal with all of the above is not to react with emotionalism, especially resentment.

Checklist

These are the key points to bear in mind when dealing with critics:

1. *Think win-win*

Conversation is first and foremost about dialogue and inclusion: you get people on your side by being on their side first. Shut down conversations where you are trying to put the other guy "down or out" and *vice-versa.*

2. Acknowledge others

Conversation is a two-way process. Immediately you cease to acknowledge the other or *vice- versa*, the conversation begins to fizzle out. Even if they do criticise you, acknowledge their opinions or point of view as a start; this does not mean you have to agree with them.

3. Be prepared to apologise

There is nothing wrong with admitting a mistake if you have made one; in that case you need to take responsibility and say you were wrong. In conversations things can get out of hand, and a few minutes later we may regret things that we just said. Apologise and resolve that you will not do it again.

4. "Call out" a person, if required

You can have a person who is not listening to you, not paying attention, is distracted by their mobile phone, *etc.* You need to make it clear to them why their behaviour is inappropriate. If they continue, then it is best to walk away from that situation.

5. Be tactful at all times

Being diplomatic in a conflict or tense moment will move the conversation forward. Always stay in a positive mood and do not let critics get you down. Do not criticise people just because they criticise you.

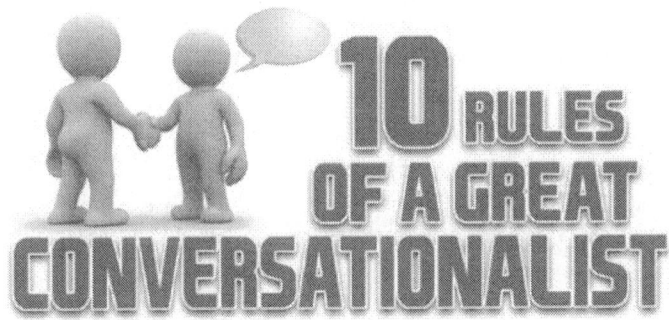

10 RULES OF A GREAT CONVERSATIONALIST

1. **BE GENUINELY INTERESTED in the person.** Strive to know more about him/her through the conversation.

2. **Focus on THE POSITIVES.** Opt for positive and meaningful topics over negative ones.

3. **CONVERSE, not debate (or argue).** Where there are differences, agree to disagree.

4. **RESPECT; don't impose, criticize, or judge.** Respect others' space and right to their views.

5. **Put the person in his/her BEST LIGHT.** Make the person look good (without being unauthentic).

6. **EMBRACE DIFFERENCES while building on commonalities.**

7. **Be TRUE TO YOURSELF.** Don't mime; be ready to share your own thoughts.

8. **50-50 SHARING.** Don't dominate the discussion. At the same time, don't hold back from sharing either.

9. **Ask PURPOSEFUL QUESTIONS.** "What drives you in life? What are your current goals? What inspired you to make this change?" Meaningful questions elicit meaningful answers.

10. **GIVE and TAKE.** Don't be too critical over what others say/do. Always give others the benefit of the doubt.

291

30. Conclusion

Conversation is a win-win game that we should all enjoy playing! It is the social "glue" that bonds us.

If you want to improve your conversational skills, know that no "magic pill" exists that will transform you into a master conversationalist overnight. You need to get serious about it and *take action*.

This action must take the form of:

(a)   Preparation
       e.g. research, reading.

(b)   Experience in the field
       i.e. going out and actually meeting new people to converse with.

You will know that your conversational skills have improved when people are attracted to you when you talk and become absorbed into what you say; your words are "gold" or "music to their ears".

First show a genuine interest in getting to know people; they will respond in kind. Always seek breadth and depth in your choice of conversational topics; steer clear of predictability. Talking too much about just one topic will bore most people; but equally, jumping around too quickly across too many topics will be too hard to follow, making your conversation appear chaotic.

Enjoy the process of conversing for its own sake: avoid trying to impose a preconceived outcome. Whoever you may converse with, speak to them for the sheer joy of it. Aim to give mutual pleasure, rather than exploiting it to get something out of it just for yourself.

Always maintain relaxed attitude, a clear voice and tonality, and a neat, smart appearance. Cultivate your "inner listener" and don't interrupt others; give everyone a chance to speak.

The inner-game is essential and must never be underestimated. It is like an aura: invisible yet present everywhere at all times. It is pointless to become outer-game knowledgeable, then sit in a corner in a social gathering and unable to use any of it. You need to be working on your inner-game in tandem.

This book is not meant to be an exercise in "learning lines"; rather, you are to absorb the principles and apply them to developing conversational routines unique to yourself.

Bearing the foregoing in mind, you will become a better conversationalist and develop yourself as a person with a stronger social circle. Conversational content is constantly overflowing in everything around us – people, places, animals, nature, things. There are no limits to what you can do with conversation; the only limiting factor is in your own mind.

Above all seek constantly to:

- Widen your skillset
  This means not just trying out one or two things, but going for variety, having a willingness to learn more and becoming proficient at many different things, and

- Get out of your comfort zone
  This means aiming for expansion and growth, happily accepting challenges and putting ourselves into new situations in life.

Happy conversing!

Contact

Your views and opinions are always most welcome. Please do contact me and let me know if you think certain topics could have been included.

My website is:

www.conversation-confidence.com

My email address is:

info@conversation-confidence.com

Acknowledgements

I would like to thank the following persons for their unique and valuable contributions:

Guido Reinke of Gold Rush Publishing for facilitating the publication of this book.

Jerry Bains for proof-reading and editing the content.

Juliet Doyle for layout and typography.

Sandra Perry for the outer cover design.

Joanna Knott for the inner cover design.

Ian Rowland for providing valuable insights into cold-reading.

Spiritual leaders around the world – too many to name, regrettably – for helping me improve my inner game.

All the people I have met and talked to over the years, from countries all around the world, who have helped me improve my conversational skills.

The Community and its members for showing me the light.

Picture references

I would also like to acknowledge the following sources of the pictures and images in this book, which have added value to and enhanced the text:

Page 4 http://izquotes.com/
Page 7 http://www.istockphoto.com
Page 8 http://www.musik-therapie.at/PederHill/

Page 11 (top) Google images
Page 11 (bottom) Google images
Page 12 http://www.norwichadvertiser24.co.uk/
Page 13 http://4photos.net/en
Page 14 http://tlc.howstuffworks.com/family/
Page 22 http://uncleeddiestheorycorner.blogspot.co.uk/
Page 23 http://skollworldforum.org/2012
Page 25 http://www.istockphoto.com
Page 26 http://www.istockphoto.com
Page 27 http://2kings4.net/
Page 31 http://www.istockphoto.com
Page 33 http://www.beyond-black-friday.com/
Page 39 http://moorstation.org/typoasis/
Page 41 Artist J J Kirby
Page 43 http://www.loriwatson.co.uk/
Page 45 Three Stooges
Page 48 Google images
Page 49 http://failposters.com/
Page 51 Google images
Page 53 Google images
Page 54 Google images
Page 55 http://fearlessmen.com/
Page 57 http://thefrogman.me/
Page 59 http://www.123rf.com/
Page 60 Google images
Page 64 http://www.imvu.com/
Page 70 http://www.istockphoto.com
Page 74 http://www.huffingtonpost.com/jerry-weissman/ and
        Warner Bros Inc. for the image
Page 78 http://www.istockphoto.com
Page 85 http://www.istockphoto.com
Page 92 http://www.scottmcarter.com/
Page 93 http://www.flickr.com/photos/lunchbreath/
Page 99 Taken on my Samsung camera
Page 100 Taken on my Samsung camera
Page 101 Taken on my Samsung camera
Page 103 http://midtel.net
Page 104 (top) Taken on my Samsung camera
Page 104 (bottom) Taken on my Samsung camera
Page 105 http://www.thespoiler.co.uk/
Page 110 Google images
Page 120 http://muddyfarmwife.blogspot.co.uk/

Page 121 Google images
Page 124 http://www.blackfoxmetalcraft.co.uk/
Page 126 http://openphoto.net/gallery/
Page 127 http://i.imgur.com/H7gkm.jpg
Page 134 http://www.elisabethhubert.com/
Page 137 Walt Disney Inc
Page 140 http://tanyaanurag.blogspot.co.uk/
Page 143 (top) Google images
Page 143 (bottom) Google images
Page 145 http://www.investopedia.com/
Page 146 http://www.edrawsoft.com/
Page 147 School Specialty Publishing (USA) now known as Carson Dellosa
Page 148 http://heightstechnology.edublogs.org/
Page 152 http://jerz.setonhill.edu/
Page 155 http://www.makanyane.com/
Page 164 Google images
Page 165 http://www.birdforum.net/
Page 168 Google images
Page 171 Google images
Page 173 http://www.teinteresasaber.com
Page 174 http://www.howstuffworks.com/
Page 189 Taken on my Samsung camera
Page 191 Cosmopolitan magazine
Page 194 Cosmopolitan magazine
Page 198 (top) http://www.shakespeares-sonnets.com/
Page 198 (bottom) http://www.biography.com/
Page 199 Taken on my Samsung camera
Page 200 Taken on my Samsung camera
Page 202 Taken on my Samsung camera
Page 203 (top) London Transport Museum
Page 203 (bottom) http://muymia.com/
Page 204 Covent garden authority
Page 206 Taken on my Samsung camera
Page 208 http://thefunkytruth.wordpress.com/
Page 211 (top) London Olympics Authority
Page 211 (bottom) London Olympics Authority
Page 212 (top) London Olympics Authority
Page 212 (bottom) London Olympics Authority
Page 213 London Olympics Authority
Page 215 (top) http://commons.wikimedia.org/
Page 215 (bottom) http://www.camdenlock.net/
Page 216 (top) Taken on my Samsung camera

Page 216 (bottom) Taken on my Samsung camera
Page 217 (top) Taken on my Samsung camera
Page 217 (bottom) Taken on my Samsung camera
Page 218 Taken on my Samsung camera
Page 219 Taken on my Samsung camera
Page 220 Taken on my Samsung camera
Page 221 http://www.streetsensation.co.uk/
Page 222 http://quittea.com/wp-content
Page 224 http://buzz.greatfxbusinesscards.com/
Page 226 http://blakeflannery.hubpages.com/
Page 231 http://www.kordellnorton.com/
Page 234 http://www.levelupliving.com/
Page 236 http://mercyness.blogspot.co.uk/
Page 238 http://www.tqsmagazine.co.uk/
Page 239 http://langwitches.org/blog/
Page 241 http://cyber-nation.com
Page 244 Google images
Page 245 http://www.wired.com/
Page 246 http://www.thepersonalistproject.org
Page 248 http://www.istockphoto.com
Page 250 http://www.idlehearts.com/
Page 251 http://quixoteconsulting.com/Blog/
Page 252 http://www.lesproctordirect.com/
Page 254 http://blog.blogcatalog.com/
Page 255 Artist Ron Leishman
Page 257 http://www.quotesvalley.com/
Page 259 http://nubiagroup.blogspot.co.uk/
Page 260 Google images
Page 263 http://charginglife.com
Page 264 http://500confessions.com/
Page 266 http://swensoncounseling.blogspot.co.uk/
Page 267 http://www.bodylanguagefordummies.com/
Page 270 http://mslangleysyear11englishclass.wikispaces.com/
Page 271 http://voodooboutique.typepad.com/
Page 273 Google images
Page 276 http://icanhas.cheezburger.com/
Page 277 http://edgeofstretch.wordpress.com/
Page 278 http://www.mdp.state.md.us/
Page 281 Google images
Page 291 http://personalexcellence.co/blog/

23007736R00163

Made in the USA
Charleston, SC
07 October 2013